SCHOLASTIC

Instant Word Lists
for Teaching Reading
and Writing

EILEEN THOMPSON
& GENE PANHORST

New York • Toronto • London • Auckland • Sydney
Mexico City • New Delhi • Hong Kong • Buenos Aires

Teaching *Resources*

Editor: Mela Ottaiano
Cover design by Maria Lilja
Interior design by Kelli Thompson

ISBN-13: 978-0-439-59025-9
ISBN-10: 0-439-59025-6

Copyright © 2008 by e² Publishing Services, LLC
All rights reserved. Published by Scholastic Inc.
Printed in the U.S.A.

1 2 3 4 5 6 7 8 9 10   40   15 14 13 12 11 10 09 08

Contents

Contents

Introduction

Have you ever found yourself in a situation where you need extra words to enhance your day-to-day curriculum? With so many words to choose from, where do you start? *Instant Word Lists for Teaching Reading and Writing* is the book for you. This time-saving resource contains dozens and dozens of word lists to supplement the language concepts you teach as part of your language arts curriculum. You can dip into the word lists to create instant word charts and enrich reading and writing lessons. The lists can also help you prepare students for the vocabulary development standards assessed on standardized tests, such as understanding the origins of words, knowing the multiple meanings of words, and recognizing different shades of meaning. Each of the word lists includes easy, target, and challenge versions that allow you to address the different ability levels within your classroom.

Chapter 1 focuses on words that cause problems. These words may look alike, sound alike, have irregular forms, or not sound as they are spelled. Using context clues and choosing the meaning that fits the context are excellent skills to reinforce as students learn more about homophones, homographs, and commonly confused words. You can discuss grammar, phonics, and letter-sound correspondence as students learn more about irregular words.

Chapter 2 focuses on developing vocabulary by building new words, shortening words, and understanding the history of words. The extensive lists of prefixes, suffixes, and roots—from Greek, Latin, and Old English—will assist you as you teach students to use word parts to understand unfamiliar words.

The lists of abbreviations, acronyms, and initialisms show how language changes over time as longer words are shortened. In addition, the lists showing how words are derived from literature and the names of people, places, wars, and so on, will help you address word-origin standards and bring home to students the rich history of the English language.

Chapter 3 expands the understanding of the history of English by focusing on words and phrases derived from other languages. Twenty other languages are represented, enriching students' knowledge of the influence of other languages on English and further helping you to address word-origin standards. You will also find an extensive collection of Spanish-English cognates.

Chapter 4 focuses on the differences between words. Because English has its roots in so many sources, it contains many words for the same thing, such as "childish" with a Greek suffix and "immature" with a Latin prefix. There are also dozens of idioms, or phrases not meant literally. Overall, the lists in this chapter help you address the importance of avoiding tired words and choosing the best word or phrase to make meaning clear when speaking or writing.

Chapter 5 focuses on jargon and other technical language. It provides lists of words used in different professions. These lists help students understand that some words have special meanings that are different from their everyday meanings.

For example, the noun *beat* is usually understood as the regular rhythm of a piece of music or of one's heart. However, the area or subject that a newspaper reporter covers is also called a *beat*.

Introduction

As you use this book, here are some activities you can do to reinforce the lists:

- After using a list, have students hunt for interesting words (and phrases) that they see in newspapers, magazines, or online. Add words students find to running lists you keep on the bulletin board. Suggest that students categorize these words, using vocabulary terms such as "jargon," "euphemism," "acronym," and so on.

- Create word puzzles for different types of lists. For example, you might create crossword puzzles for words from mythology and word searches for words with silent letters. Encourage your students to create their own puzzles to challenge their classmates. Several puzzle-generating programs are available on the Internet, such as http://puzzlemaker.com.

- Start collecting idioms and other examples of wordplay, such as puns and clichés. Students can illustrate these in literal and/or figurative ways. Also challenge students to create illustrations using homophones, homographs, and commonly confused words.

- Bring in examples of graphic novels. Have students discuss the effect of onomatopoeia. Invite them to create graphics using onomatopoeia.

Chapter 1

Words That Cause Problems

> "My students are often confused by homophones they read. I need more examples than the ones provided in my textbook."

There are many types of words in English that can be difficult to learn and remember. These tricky words may sound alike (homophones), look alike (homographs, or even similar words such as *conscience* and *conscious*), have irregular forms (such as certain verbs or plural nouns), or not sound as they are spelled (often due to silent letters).

Having a dictionary or thesaurus on hand is always helpful when trying to determine the meaning of a word. However, using context clues to select the meaning that best fits that context is an excellent skill to reinforce as students learn more about homophones, homographs, commonly confused words, and so on. Remind students that the context of a word includes all the other words, phrases, clauses, and sentences around it.

You may also want to suggest that students tackle commonly confused words by writing a single sentence that contains any word set presenting a problem. For example, for *costume/custom*: He wears a festive costume (clothing) during celebrations because it is the custom (tradition or usual practice) in his country. This can later act as a mnemonic device when students encounter the words again.

HOMOPHONES

Homophones are words that sound alike but are spelled differently and have different meanings.

Easy

A

aid	help
aide	assistant

ail	be sick
ale	a drink

ate	past tense of *eat*
eight	one more than seven

aye	yes
eye	an organ for sight

B

bare	not covered
bear	a large animal

be	to exist
bee	an insect

beat	to hit or defeat
beet	a vegetable

been	past participle of *be*
bin	a container

blew	past tense of *blow*
blue	a color

brake	part of a machine that slows it down
break	smash

bread	a food made with flour, water, and yeast
bred	past tense of *breed*

C

capital	seat of government
capitol	building where state legislature meets

cell	room in a prison
sell	offer for sale

cellar	basement
seller	a person selling something

cent	100th of a dollar
scent	odor
sent	past tense of *send*

cents	pennies
scents	odors

cheap	not expensive
cheep	sound made by young bird

chews	grinds up food
choose	pick

creak	squeak
creek	a stream

D

dear	someone loved
deer	an animal

dew	moisture
do	perform

die	stop living
dye	coloring

E

ewe	a female sheep
you	pronoun that refers to the person being addressed (I'm speaking to you)

F

fair	just, not biased
fare	amount charged for a trip

flour	a powder made from grain
flower	blossom

for	a preposition
fore	the front of something
four	the number after three

G

gnu an African antelope
knew past tense of *know*
new opposite of old

groan moan
grown past participle of *grow*

H

hair fine strands growing on head and skin
hare an animal resembling a rabbit

hay dried grass
hey informal greeting

heal to make healthy again
heel back part of foot

hear to perceive sound
here this place

hi informal greeting
high far above the ground

hole a hollow space
whole complete

hour 60 minutes
our belonging to us

I

in the opposite of out
inn a tavern or small hotel

its belonging to it
it's contraction of *it is*

K

knight in medieval Europe, a soldier on horseback
night the opposite of day

knot something you tie in a rope or string
not no way

know to be aware of; to have learned
no the opposite of yes

L

lie to recline
lye a strong substance used for cleaning

M

made the past tense of *make*
maid a housekeeper

mail letters and other items sent by post
male not female

main chief; most important
Maine one of the 50 states
mane the hair on the head and neck of a lion or horse

O

oar a paddle; something you row with
or a conjunction

one the number between zero and two
won past tense of *win*

P

pail a bucket
pale light; lacking color

pair two of a kind
pear a fruit

peace calm; quiet; a period without war
piece a part of something

pray to speak to God; to request or beg
prey someone or something that is hunted

principal the head of a school
principle a rule or standard

R

rap to knock
wrap to cover with paper or cloth

read the past tense of the verb *read*; found meaning in written words
red a color

right correct
wright someone who makes or repairs something
write to compose or put words on paper

road a path
rode past tense of *ride*
rowed past tense of *row*; paddled

role	a part played by an actor	**some**	not all		**W**		
roll	to move on wheels	**sum**	the total		**wait**	to delay or slow down for someone
		son	a male child		**weight**	how heavy something is
rose	a flower	**sun**	the star around which Earth rotates			
rows	paddles a boat				**war**	conflict
					wore	past tense of *wear*; had on
S		**T**				
sail	strong cloth on a boat that catches the wind and helps the boat move	**tail**	the section at the rear end of an animal's body		**ware**	something you sell
					wear	to put or have on
sale	a bargain; selling goods for money	**tale**	a story		**where**	at what place
sea	the ocean	**to**	a preposition showing direction		**we**	I and one or more people
see	to perceive through the use of the eyes	**too**	also		**wee**	little
		two	the number between one and three			
					weak	not strong
seam	the place where two pieces of cloth are joined	**toad**	a tailless creature that resembles a frog		**week**	seven days
seem	to appear to be	**towed**	past tense of *tow*; dragged away		**wood**	timber
					would	is or was willing to
sew	to use thread to join pieces of cloth; to mend	**toe**	part of the foot			
so	therefore; as a result	**tow**	to drag away			

Target

A		**altar**	a table or other raised structure used for religious ceremonies		**bark**	the outer covering of a tree
air	a mixture of gases that we breath	**alter**	change		**barque**	a small sailing ship
heir	someone who inherits				**baron**	a nobleman
		B			**barren**	empty
aisle	a passageway	**bail**	money paid to release someone from prison temporarily		**base**	bottom of something
I'll	I will				**bass**	deep voice
isle	a small island	**bale**	a bundle of hay			

beach	sandy shore	**cereal**	a breakfast food	**crews**	groups of people working on a ship or who perform a similar task
beech	a type of tree	**serial**	a story published in installments (one part at a time)	**cruise**	a journey by boat
berth	a bed on a ship or train			**cue**	a prompt or signal to do something
birth	the beginning of life	**chute**	a passage or shaft	**queue**	a line of people
billed	sent a statement of charges	**shoot**	to fire or discharge	**currant**	a type of fruit
build	to construct			**current**	up-to-date
boar	a male hog	**cite**	to name or mention	**cymbal**	a musical instrument
bore	to make someone lose interest	**sight**	the ability to see	**symbol**	a sign
		site	a place or location		
board	a piece of wood			**D**	
bored	not interested	**clause**	a group of words with a subject and predicate	**days**	periods of time made up of 24 hours; plural of day
born	brought into existence; given life	**claws**	the curved nails of an animal	**daze**	a state of confusion
borne	past participle of *bear*				
		coarse	rough; not smooth	**doe**	a female deer
borough	part of a large city	**course**	a path or route	**dough**	mixture of flour, water, and other ingredients
burro	a small donkey				
burrow	a small hole in which an animal lives	**colonel**	a military officer		
		kernel	a grain of cereal	**dual**	double; with two parts
brews	prepares a drink			**duel**	a fight with swords
bruise	a damaged and discolored area on the skin	**complement**	to go well with or add to		
		compliment	praise	**E**	
bridal	relating to a wedding			**earn**	to make money
bridle	leather straps to control a horse	**coop**	a pen or cage	**urn**	a vase
		coupe	a car		
but	except			**eaves**	part of a roof that sticks out over the wall that supports it
butt	to hit or push	**core**	center; main		
		corps	a military unit or other group of people	**eves**	plural of *eve*; the day or night just before an important holiday or festival (New Year's Eve)
C					
cache	a stockpile	**council**	an assembly or committee		
cash	money	**counsel**	to advise		

F

faint   to pass out
feint   to pretend

faun   a mythological creature with the body of a man and the horns and legs of a goat
fawn   a young deer

feat   a great and courageous deed
feet   the plural of *foot*

flair   style
flare   to burn brightly

flea   a bug
flee   to leave quickly

flew   the past tense of *fly*
flu   short for *influenza*, an infectious viral disease
flue   a chimney or other outlet to carry smoke

G

gait   a way of walking or running
gate   a type of door or other moveable barrier

genes   units that carry a person's hereditary characteristics
jeans   dungarees; pants made of denim

gilt   a thin coating of gold
guilt   a feeling that you did something wrong

grate   to grind and shred, such as to grate cheese
great   excellent; very large

grater   a device for grinding and shredding
greater   bigger or mightier

grease   a fatty or oily substance
Greece   a country in south-east Europe

H

hail   frozen rain
hale   in good health

hall   a corridor or passageway
haul   to carry

heard   past tense of *hear*
herd   a group of cattle

higher   farther above the ground than something else
hire   to employ

hoarse   sounding rough and croaky
horse   an animal

I

idle   not working; lazy
idol   something or someone worshipped and adored
idyll   a peaceful, happy time or experience

J

jam   a fruit spread
jamb   part of a window or door frame

K

knead   to press or work dough to make a smooth mass
need   to require

L

lain   past participle of *lie*
lane   a path or narrow road

leak   an opening from which water drips
leek   a vegetable similar to an onion

lessen   to reduce or make less
lesson   something you learn

liar   someone who tells a lie
lyre   a musical instrument you play by plucking the strings

links   connections
lynx   a wildcat

load   a burden; something carried from place to place
lode   a deposit of ore

loan   an amount of money you borrow with the promise to pay it back
lone   single; only

loot booty; plunder
lute a musical instrument similar to a guitar

M

mall a shopping center
maul to tear or attack

marshal a law enforcement officer
martial soldierly; military

mat a pad or small carpet
matte dull; not shiny

Mays more than one month of May
maze a labyrinth; a confusing network of passages

meat the flesh of an animal
meet to encounter; to get together
mete to give out or distribute

medal an award or badge of honor
meddle to intrude or get in the way

might power or strength
mite a bug

miner someone who works in a mine
minor a juvenile

moor to tie up or fasten an object such as a boat
more additional

moose a large animal in the deer family
mousse a chilled dessert similar to pudding

morn a shortened form of morning; the time period before noon
mourn to grieve for and feel sad

morning the time period before noon
mourning grief; sorrow

muscle a bundle of fibers in the body that contributes to movement and strength
mussel a type of marine creature with a shell

N

naval referring to the navy
navel a small hollow in the abdomen

O

ode a type of poem
owed required to pay someone else

overdo to go beyond or do too much
overdue late; tardy

P

pain hurt; ache
pane the glass part of a window or door

pause to stop briefly
paws the feet of an animal

peak the highest point
peek to take a brief look
pique temper; wounded pride

peal the ringing or clanging of bells
peel to take away the skin or outer covering

pedal the part of a bike or car that you operate with your feet
peddle to sell

peer to look at something closely and carefully
pier a platform jutting out over the water

plain simple
plane a flat surface

pleas cries for aid
please to satisfy or make happy

poor not wealthy
pore a tiny opening or hole, particularly in the skin
pour to rain heavily

pride strong feeling of self-worth
pried past tense of *pry*; forced open

profit money made; benefit
prophet someone who tells the future or speaks for a deity

Q

quarts   more than one quart
quartz   a mineral

R

rain   water falling from clouds; precipitation
reign   to rule over as a monarch
rein   a strap for controlling a horse

raise   to lift
rays   beams of light
raze   to destroy or tear down

raiser   something or someone that raises something
razor   a sharp tool for shaving

read   to interpret written words
reed   a slender stalk of grass

real   actual; genuine
reel   a spool

recede   to pull back or move away
reseed   to plant seeds again

review   to examine
revue   a type of variety show

ring   a circular band
wring   to twist or squeeze

roomer   a person who rents a room in a house
rumor   gossip; a story passed from person to person

root   the part of a plant that spreads underground
route   a path or course

rote   memorized
wrote   past tense of *write*; composed

rung   past tense of *ring*; made a bell sound
wrung   past tense of *wring*; squeezed

S

soar   to glide or fly
sore   painful; tender

scene   sight; setting
seen   past participle of *see*; perceived

shake   to mix by moving back and forth quickly; to tremble
sheik   a leader of a group of Arabs

shear   to cut hair or fleece
sheer   very thin and fine

shone   past tense of *shine*; glowed brightly
shown   past tense of *show*; displayed

side   surface or face
sighed   past tense of *sigh*; exhaled noisily

slay   to kill
sleigh   a vehicle pulled over snow or ice by a horse

stair   a step or flight of steps
stare   to look intensely at something

stake   a post driven into the ground
steak   a thick slice of meat

stationary   not moving
stationery   paper used for correspondence

steal   to take something that doesn't belong to you
steel   a metal; a strong alloy of iron and carbon

straight   not crooked
strait   a channel or narrow body of water

suite   a group of rooms
sweet   sugary

sundae   an ice-cream dessert
Sunday   a day of the week

T

teas   plural of *tea*; drinks made from leaves of a tea plant
tease   to kid or mock
tees   plural of *tee*; pegs used to hold golf balls

their	belonging to them
there	at that place or point
they're	they are
threw	past tense of *throw*; tossed
through	from one side to the other
throne	a chair for royalty
thrown	past participle of *throw*; was tossed
thyme	a spice
time	moment; instance
tide	the ebb and flow of the ocean
tied	past tense of *tie*; fastened
tighten	to make tighter
titan	a person of extraordinary achievement

U

undo	take apart; cancel
undue	too much

V

vain	conceited
vane	a flat metal blade that turns in the wind
vein	a blood vessel

vale	a valley
veil	sheer fabric covering the face

W

wade	to walk through shallow water
weighed	past tense of *weigh*; measured how heavy something is
wail	to moan or cry out in pain
whale	a large marine mammal
waist	the middle part of the body
waste	to not use properly; to squander
way	a path
weigh	to measure how heavy something is
whey	the watery liquid that separates from milk and is used to make cheese
weather	the temperature and other atmospheric conditions
whether	if
weave	to make cloth
we've	we have

we'd	we had or we would
weed	a wild plant that people want to get rid of
which	what one
witch	a make-believe person with super-natural powers
whine	to complain or cry
wine	an alcoholic drink made from grapes
whoa	stop
woe	trouble and sorrow
whose	belonging to whom
who's	who is
wind	to turn or twist
wined	gave wine to

Y

you're	you are
your	belonging to you
yoke	a wooden frame or harness
yolk	the yellow part of an egg

Challenge

A

aerie	an eagle's nest
airy	open and spacious
aural	relating to the ear or hearing
oral	spoken

B

bait	a lure; something to attract a fish or other animal
bate	lessen; lower
baize	a coarse woolen or cotton cloth
bays	areas by the sea
bask	lie in the warmth of the sun
Basque	an ethnic group living in the Pyrenees mountains in north-central Spain and southwestern France
beer	an alcoholic drink
bier	a table holding a casket or dead body
bite	to tear with your teeth
byte	in computing, a set of bits, or units of memory
bloc	a union of countries
block	a large, solid piece
bootee or bootie	a baby's knit boot
booty	loot

broach to mention or bring up a topic
brooch a pin used as jewelry

burger a meat patty
burgher a comfortable, middle-class citizen; in medieval Europe, a merchant

C

canon	an approved set of writings
cannon	a weapon or big gun
canvas	a heavy fabric
canvass	to campaign or drum up support
carat	a unit used to measure precious stones such as diamonds
caret	a mark showing where something belongs
carrot	a root vegetable
carol	a song
carrel	a small partitioned work space
cast	to throw
caste	a social class determined by birth
cede	to yield or give up
seed	something you plant to grow plants

censer a container for burning incense
censor a person who examines material to remove anything considered offensive
sensor a device that senses light, movement, or temperature change

chord two or more musical notes played together
cord string or thin rope

click to make a sharp, short sound
clique a close group or circle of friend

complacent smug or self-satisfied
complaisant behaving in a way that will please others

cygnet a baby swan
signet a small seal (a signet ring)

D

ducked got down quickly to avoid being hit or seen
duct a pipe or tube through which something flows

F

faze	to bother or disturb
phase	a period of time; a stage
foreword	a preface or intro-duction
forward	ahead; onward

G

gamble	to bet money or property
gambol	to frolic or move about playfully
gorilla	a large ape
guerilla	a fighter; a member of an irregular or paramilitary group that operates in small bands

H

hoard	to save up
horde	a large group of people
holy	sacred
wholly	totally; completely
hostel	an inexpensive inn
hostile	not friendly; showing anger

K

key	something for unlocking a door
quay	a dock or jetty

L

leach	to slowly take something away
leech	a blood-sucking creature
lean	to bend over or tilt
lien	the legal right to take or hold property as security against a debt
levee	an embankment for preventing flooding
levy	to impose a tax

M

mantel	a frame around or shelf above a fireplace
mantle	the part of Earth between the crust and the core
mask	something covering the face to disguise a person
masque	a type of play with masked performers
mean	not nice
mien	manner, appearance, and bearing
mews	an area with streets that once had stables but now has housing for people
muse	an inspiration

P

palate	the top of the mouth
palette	an artist's tray for mixing paints
pallet	a narrow hard bed
plait	a braid
plate	a dish
plum	a fruit
plumb	a lead weight at the end of a line
psalter	a book containing psalms
salter	a person who sells salt

R

rancor	bitterness; resentment
ranker	someone who ranks things
rapped	tapped; knocked
rapt	enthralled; completely caught up in
wrapped	covered with paper or cloth
reek	to stink or smell strongly
wreak	to bring about; to cause
rest	to take it easy or relax
wrest	to gain with difficulty; to seize
rye	a cereal grain or grass
wry	having a dry wit; ironic

s

sachet	a small pouch of scented powder or potpourri
sashay	to sway or glide
scull	a small racing boat
skull	the bony framework of the head
sear	to burn or scorch
seer	a fortune teller
serf	a peasant who worked the land in feudal Europe
surf	waves
serge	a type of cloth usually made from wool
surge	to rush forward
shier	more shy or bashful
shire	a district
sign	a poster or mark
sine	a geometric function
sink	to go down
sync or synch	shortened form of synchronization; harmony; causing things to happen at the same time

staid	settled; dull
stayed	past tense of *stay*; remained
step	one raised platform in a set of stairs
steppe	a very large plain without trees
stolen	past participle of *steal*; taken without permission
stollen	a sweet fruitbread that originated in Germany

T

tacked	past tense of *tack*; fastened with a small nail
tact	skill and consideration in dealing with others
taper	a tall, slender candle
tapir	a large hoofed animal
team	a group working together
teem	to pour or be full of
tear	a droplet of water from the eye
tier	a row or level

tic	a twitch or sudden contraction of the muscles
tick	a clicking sound
timber	wood; lumber
timbre	a quality of a sound
tort	a wrongful act
torte	a rich cake
tracked	past tense of *track*; followed
tract	an expanse of land
troop	a group of people with a similar purpose
troupe	a company of actors

V

vial	a small bottle used for medicine
vile	disgusting; evil

W

waive	to give up or put aside
wave	a ripple or upward thrust of water
wet	not dry
whet	to sharpen

HOMOGRAPHS

Homographs are words that are spelled alike, but have different word origins and different meanings. You see them listed as separate entries in the dictionary. (Starred words are also pronounced differently.)

Easy

A

arm	to give someone a weapon
arm	a body part

B

ball	a round object
ball	a formal party
band	a group of musicians
band	a strip often used to hold things together
bank	a place to keep money
bank	a slope of land leading down to water
bark	a loud sound made by a dog
bark	the rough outer covering of a tree
bat	a wooden stick
bat	a flying mammal that comes out at night
bill	a bird's beak
bill	a check or list showing how much money is owed
box	a container
box	to fight with the fists

C

calf	a young cow
calf	the back of a person's leg between the knee and ankle
can	a container
can	is able to
close*	nearby
close*	to shut

D

date	a fruit
date	a day, month, and year
dear	someone loved or valued
dear	a salutation in a letter
does*	performs; acts
does*	more than one doe, or female deer
dove*	a type of bird
dove*	past tense of *dive*; went under water
duck	a swimming bird
duck	to get down quickly in order to avoid being hit or seen

F

fair	pleasing; just
fair	a market; a gathering to celebrate an event

L

lie	to recline or stretch out
lie	to tell a falsehood
live*	not dead
live*	to pass through life; to be alive

M

mine	something belonging to me
mine	an excavation made in the earth for the purpose of extracting minerals

P

pen	an enclosed area where an animal is confined
pen	a writing instrument
pit	a hole in the ground
pit	the stone-like object in a fruit

pound	a unit of weight
pound	a place where animals are kept
pound	to beat

R

ring	a circular band
ring	to sound a bell
rose	the past tense of *rise*
rose	a flower

| row | a series of objects placed next to each other |
| row | to use paddles to move a boat |

S

| saw | a tool with a jagged edge |
| saw | past tense of *see*; perceived |

seal	a marine mammal
seal	to close
shed	a small building for storage
shed	to lose or get rid of

W

| well | healthy |
| well | a hole from which water is drawn |

Target

A

| affect* | to have an effect on |
| affect* | to take on airs or pretend to be something |

B

bail	money paid for the temporary release of a prisoner from jail
bail	to remove water from a boat
base	bottom; stand
base	vile; corrupt; contemptible
bass*	a fish
bass*	a low-pitched sound
batter	someone who hits a ball
batter	a partially liquid mixture used to bake cakes

bay	an area of the sea partly enclosed by land
bay	a small evergreen tree
bay	to howl
bay	a reddish-brown horse
bear	a large furry animal
bear	to endure
blow	to breathe hard on something
blow	sudden, unexpected bad luck
bluff	to pretend
bluff	a cliff
boil	to heat in order to change from liquid to gas
boil	a painful sore filled with pus
bore	to pierce
bore	to make someone uninterested; to tire mentally

bound	to spring upward or jump
bound	past tense of *bind*; tied up
bound	limit or boundary (often plural)
bound	headed in a certain direction
brush	to clean or groom
brush	a thick growth of bushes

C

cape	an outer garment without sleeves
cape	a spit of land projecting into the water
case	a box; a container
case	a set of circumstances (the case against someone)
chaff	part of grains of wheat
chaff	to poke fun at

chap   a boy or man
chap   to redden, harden, split, and become sore

chest   upper body; torso
chest   a container; a box for storage

commune*   a place where people live supporting each other
commune*   to talk together

content*   happy; satisfied
content*   everything contained in something

converse*   opposite; contrary
converse*   to have a conversation with

corn   a vegetable with kernels on long ears
corn   a hardening of the skin on the toe

court   to date; to woo
court   a yard

cue   a signal or prompt
cue   a long rod for playing pool

curry   a highly spiced dish
curry   to groom a horse

D

desert*   a large expanse of arid land
desert*   to abandon

down   opposite of up
down   the soft feathers of a young bird

F

felt   past tense of *feel*; touched
felt   a matted fabric

fine   in good condition
fine   money paid as a penalty

firm   solid; compact
firm   a group of people selling goods and services

G

game   something you play
game   wild animals

grate   to shred
grate   a framework of metal bars covering an opening

J

jam   a fruit spread
jam   to push things together

junk   worthless things
junk   a flat-bottomed sailing boat

K

kind   warm; generous
kind   type; category

M

match   a contest
match   a stick with a tip you can light

might   force
might   maybe

mint   a flavorful plant
mint   a place where coins are made

mold   to shape
mold   fungus

P

pad   a small, thin cushion
pad   to move on foot

page   one side of a piece of paper
page   to summon someone

palm   the inner side of the hand
palm   a tree, or a leaf from a palm tree

pants   breathes heavily
pants   trousers

peer   to look closely
peer   an equal

perch   a freshwater fish
perch   a rod or stick on which a bird sits

pitch   a dark, sticky substance like tar
pitch   to throw

plane   an aircraft
plane   a carpenter's tool

pool   a place for swimming
pool   a form of billiards

pore   a tiny opening
pore   to read carefully

press   to bear down or squeeze
press   to force into military service

R

rare   unusual
rare   cooked so that the inside is still red (a rare steak)

rash   hasty
rash   a red, itchy skin condition

root   the part of a plant that grows underground
root   to dig or rummage through something
root   to cheer on

S

school   a place for learning
school   a group of fish

sound   noise; something you hear
sound   solid; well thought out; in good condition
sound   a wide ocean inlet
sound   to probe or measure the depth of water

spell   to name the letters of a word
spell   a short period
spell   words spoken to make magic

squash   a gourd
squash   a game similar to handball but played with a racket

stole   a shawl
stole   past tense of *steal*; took something that didn't belong to you

T

tarry*   covered with tar
tarry*   to delay; to stay somewhere temporarily

tear*   a drop of fluid from the eye
tear*   to pull apart

temple   each side of the head along the forehead
temple   a place of worship

tense   worried; not relaxed
tense   how a verb expresses time

till   a cashbox
till   to prepare land for crops

tire   the rubber part of a car wheel
tire   to exhaust or wear out

toast   bread that has been heated and browned
toast   to say words to honor someone as you clink glasses and drink

toll   a charge for using a bridge or road
toll   to ring a bell

V

vault   a place where valuables are kept
vault   to leap or jump

W

wind*   moving air; a breeze
wind*   to wrap around something

wound*   an injury
wound*   past tense of *wind*

Challenge

A

adder a person who adds
adder a water snake

affected made to happen; brought about
affected pretentious

angle the space formed at the point where two lines meet
angle to scheme to get something

arch a curved structure
arch haughty

B

bisque a creamy soup
bisque a pale, yellowish color

bit a little piece
bit a unit of information on a computer
bit past tense of *bite*

broach to bring up a topic
broach to move a boat broadside to the wind or waves

buff a person with deep knowledge
buff to shine or polish

buffer someone or something that polishes
buffer a barrier that lessens the shock or affect of something

buffet* a meal of many different dishes laid out on a large table from which people serve themselves
buffet* to strike repeatedly; to batter

bumble to make a buzzing noise like a bee
bumble to act clumsily or ineptly

burden something carried or borne
burden a recurring idea or theme

burn to be on fire
burn a small stream

bustle a pad used to expand the back of a skirt
bustle to move about busily

C

caper the edible bud from a pungent plant
caper to frolic or move playfully

capital the upper part of a column
capital money; funds

card a piece of stiff paper
card to comb with a wire-toothed brush

carp a fish
carp to quibble or find fault

char a fish similar to a trout
char to burn or scorch

chop to cut into small pieces
chop to change directions suddenly

chord a line segment
chord a combination of three or more notes

chow food
chow a breed of dog

chum a pal
chum bait

cobbler a person who makes shoes or boots
cobbler a type of fruit pie

compound a mixture of two or more things
compound an enclosed area with a group of buildings in it

console* a cabinet
console* to comfort

D

deal a business transaction
deal wood from a fir or pine tree

dice game cubes
dice to chop into small pieces

die	to stop living	
die	a game cube (pl. *dice*)	

diet	food a person regularly eats
diet	a legislative body

E

egg	something laid by a bird or fish
egg	to urge someone to do something

entrance*	a door or way in
entrance*	to put in a trance or under a spell

F

fluke	a fish
fluke	something unexpected

H

haze	mist; smoke
haze	to harass someone

I

invalid*	not valid or legitimate
invalid*	a person made weak by illness

iris	a flower
iris	the colored part of the eye

K

kill	to cause something or someone to die
kill	a stream

L

lay	the past tense of *lie*; reclined
lay	to put in a particular position
lay	not a member of the clergy
lay	a narrative poem

M

mail	letters, cards, packages
mail	armor with interlocking rings

March	the third month of the year
march	to walk in line with regular movements

maroon	a purplish-red color
maroon	to leave someone behind

mean	unkind; cruel
mean	average
mean	to signify

meet	suitable; fitting
meet	to encounter someone

minute*	60 seconds
minute*	very tiny

mule	a pack animal
mule	a slipper or backless shoe

P

patter	rapid speech; chatter
patter	to make light tapping sounds

pawn	a person being used for another's purposes
pawn	to hock or borrow money against

pink	a pastel shade of red and white
pink	to cut with shears; to stab

plump	chubby
plump	to drop down heavily

pod	a casing or housing; a shell
pod	a group of marine mammals

primer*	an undercoat of paint
primer*	an elementary textbook teaching reading

Q

quarry	an animal that is hunted; prey
quarry	a pit where stone is dug out of the ground

quash	to set aside a law or ruling
quash	to put down forcibly; to suppress

R

recount*	a second counting or tallying
recount*	to tell or relate

recover	to get back
recover	to cover again

refrain	the part of a song or poem you repeat	**shock**	a thick mass (a shock of hair)	**T**		
refrain	to hold back or not do	**shock**	to surprise or disturb greatly	**tart**	sharp and sour
				tart	a type of pie
refuse*	don't accept; to decline	**see**	to perceive through the eyes	**tender**	sensitive to touch
refuse*	garbage	**see**	an area controlled by a bishop	**tender**	to make an offer in writing
rent	money paid to owner for housing			**tender**	a small boat
rent	a tear	**sheer**	thin, fine, transparent	**troll**	a make-believe creature
		sheer	to veer or swerve off course	**troll**	to drag a line through the water
resort*	a vacation place				
resort*	an option or chance	**shy**	bashful		
resort*	to sort again	**shy**	to throw or fling	**W**	
S		**spit**	a narrow body of land projecting into a body of water	**wax**	a slightly greasy substance used for polishing
shoal	shallow water	**spit**	to expel saliva	**wax**	to increase in size
shoal	a large school of fish				

WORDS PRONOUNCED DIFFERENTLY AS DIFFERENT PARTS OF SPEECH

Sometimes one word is pronounced differently when it is used as different parts of speech. This occurs most frequently with words that can be used as nouns or verbs. Often, the stress changes from one syllable to another. When this occurs, the vowel sound also changes. Sometimes, though, only the consonant sound is different. (See "Easy" words below.)

Easy

H

house (n.) (hous)	a building you live in
house (v.) (houz)	to provide a place for something to be stored or for a person to live

U

use (n.) (yoos)	purpose; function
use (v.) (yooz)	to employ something or put it in action

Target

A

a buse´ (n.)	mistreatment
a buse´ (v.)	to treat badly
al´ ter nate (adj.)	every other one
al´ ter nate (n.)	a stand-in; someone who is available to take someone else's place
al ter nate´ (v.)	to happen in turns

C

com´ bat (n.)	a battle
com bat´ (v.)	to fight
com´ pound (adj.)	made of two or more parts
com´ pound (n.)	a mixture of two or more things
com pound´ (v.)	to make something by combining two or more things

con´ duct (n.)	behavior
con duct´ (v.)	to lead; to behave
con´ flict (n.)	a struggle or fight
con flict´ (v.)	to be opposed to or contradict
con´ test (n.)	a competition
con test´ (v.)	to disapprove of or challenge something
con´ tract (n.)	an agreement
con tract´ (v.)	to form an agreement
con´ trast (n.)	difference
con trast´ (v.)	to show the difference
con´ vert (n.)	somebody who has changed from one form of belief or religion to another
con vert´ (v.)	to transform or change something from one form to another

con´ vict (n.) — a person in prison for a crime
con vict´ (v.) — to find guilty of a crime

D

de´ light (n.) — joy; pleasure
de light´ (v.) — to give pleasure to

de´ mand (n.) — a strong request
de mand´ (v.) — to request boldly and forcefully

di´ gest (n.) — a magazine made up mostly of shortened forms or summaries of articles
di gest´ (v.) — to take in and process food or ideas

E

ex´ cuse´ (n.) — reason not to do something
ex´ cuse´ (v.) — to give a reason not to do something

ex´ port (n.) — something sent outside of the country for sale
ex port´ (v.) — to send something to another country for sale

G

grad´ u ate (n.) — someone who completes a course of study at a school
grad u ate´ (v.) — to complete a course of study at a school

I

im´ port (n.) — something brought into the country
im port´ (v.) — to bring into the country

in´ sult (n.) — a disrespectful remark
in sult´ (v.) — to make a disrespectful remark

M

mo´ bile (adj.) — able to move easily
mo bile´ (n.) — a sculpture with parts that move that hangs from the ceiling

O

ob´ ject (n.) — something that can be seen and touched
ob ject´ (v.) — to oppose something

P

per´ mit (n.) — official permission or a license to do something
per mit´ (v.) — to allow something or give permission for it

pres´ ent (n.) — a gift you give to someone
pre sent´ (v.) — to give something to someone

pro´ duce (n.) — fruits and vegetables
pro duce´ (v.) — to make or create something

pro´ ject (n.) — a task that takes time and effort to complete
pro ject´ (v.) — to send forward

R

rec´ ord (n.) — an official document
re cord´ (v.) — to write down for official use

re´ bel (n.) — someone who defies authority
re bel´ (v.) — to defy authority or act in protest

re´ ject (n.) — something found unsuitable or not up to the standard
re ject´ (v.) — to turn down

re´ lay (n.) — the passing of one thing to another; a type of race
re lay´ (v.) — to send something or pass it on

re´ cess (n.) — a temporary break
re cess´ (v.) — to halt for a short period

S

se´ pa rate (adj.) — distinct
se pa rate´ (v.) — to divide

sub´ ject (n.) — a person under someone's rule or command
sub ject´ (v.) — to place under or below someone's rule or command; to inflict

sur´ vey (n.) — something you use to collect people's opinions
sur vey´ (v.) — to look at carefully or gather people's opinions

sus´ pect (n.) — somebody who is thought to be guilty of doing something illegal
sus pect´ (v.) — to think that someone is guilty

T

trans´ port (n.) — a vehicle used for carrying people or things from place to place
trans port´ (v.) — to move to another place

Challenge

A

ab´ sent (adj.) — not present
ab sent´ (v.) — to keep away

ab stract´ (adj.) — not concrete
ab´ stract (n.) — a brief statement summarizing the main ideas
ab stract´ (v.) — to take away or remove

af´ fect (n.) — a feeling, emotion, or tendency
af fect´ (v.) — to have an effect on

ad´ vo cate (n.) — a supporter
ad vo cate´ (v.) — to speak out in support

al´ ly (n.) — friend
al ly´ (v.) — join with

ar tic´ u late (adj.) — well spoken
ar tic u late´ (v.) — to voice or express yourself clearly

at´ tri bute (n.) — a quality or characteristic
at tri´ bute (v.) — to give credit to or assign a characteristic to

C

com´ bine (n.) — a machine for harvesting and threshing grain
com bine´ (v.) — to join or mix

D

de´ fect (n.) — a fault or flaw
de fect´ (v.) — to leave your country because you find fault with its government

de´ lib e rate (adj.) — carefully thought through and considered
de lib e rate´ (v.) — to consider carefully; to weigh

de´ so late (adj.)   forlorn; extremely sad and hopeless

de so late´ (v.)   to lay waste to; to bring disaster to

du´ pli cate (n.)   a copy

du pli cate´ (v.)   to make a copy

E

es´ cort (n.)   a person who accompanies or guides someone else

es cort´ (v.)   to accompany or guide

L

lam´ i nate (n.)   a product used as an outer covering

lam in nate´ (v.)   to cover with a thin sheet of something

P

per´ fect (adj.)   complete in every way; flawless

per fect´ (v.)   to make something as good as possible

R

re´ coil (n.)   the spring or kickback from a gun that is fired

re coil´ (v.)   to draw back or retreat

T

trans´ plant (n.)   an organ or other body part taken from one body and given to another

trans plant´ (v.)   to move from one place to another

COMMONLY CONFUSED WORDS

Some pairs of words are easy to confuse. In many pairs, the words sound a lot alike, although not exactly alike. In others, the meanings of the two words are close but not the same.

Easy

A

angel	a heavenly being
angle	the space formed between sides of a triangle or other geometric shape
among	used to connect three or more things
between	used to connect two things

B

borrow	to take or get something from someone on a temporary basis
lend	to give something to someone on a temporary basis

C

can	is able to
may	has permission to
costume	a disguise or special clothes
custom	a tradition

D

desert	an expanse of arid land
dessert	a sweet treat
diner	an informal restaurant or a person eating
dinner	the main meal of the day

F

few	a small number of things that can be counted (few apples)
less	a smaller part of a whole or mass (less pie)

G

good	adjective meaning satisfactory or fine
well	adverb meaning satisfactorily, comfortably, or adjective meaning healthy

L

loose	not tight
lose	to misplace or not be able to find

P

pedal	something on a car or bike you operate with your foot
petal	part of a flower

Q

quiet	without noise
quite	to a considerable extent

T

than	used after a comparative adjective or adverb (bigger than)
then	at that time; therefore
trail	to track or follow
trial	a hearing in the court of law

Target

A

accent	the individual way you pronounce a word
ascent	a climb or rise
assent	to agree to something
accept	to take or agree to
except	not including
adapt	to modify or change for a particular circumstance
adopt	to legally take into one's family
advice	counsel; suggestions for what to do
advise	to counsel someone or suggest what to do
affect	to make something happen
effect	the result
alley	a passage between buildings
ally	a friend
all ready	everyone is ready
already	by this time
allot	to give or assign; to parcel out
a lot	plenty
all together	everyone is together
altogether	totally

anxious	worried; uneasy
eager	excited; enthusiastic
award	something given as a result of a decision by judges (an award for perfect attendance)
reward	something given in return for a service (a reward for finding a lost cat)

B

bath	the act of soaking in a bathtub
bathe	to wash or cleanse yourself
bazaar	an outdoor market
bizarre	strange
beside	next to
besides	in addition
breadth	depth; expanse; span
breath	the air you inhale and exhale
breathe	to inhale and exhale air

C

calendar	a chart that shows the month and days of the year
colander	a strainer
carton	a box
cartoon	a drawing or animated film

click	a short, sharp sound
clique	a small group of close friends
cloth	fabric
clothe	to dress or put garments on
command	to lead or direct
commend	to praise
complement	to add to or complete
compliment	praise or flattery
conscience	sense of what is right and wrong
conscious	aware
convince	to lead someone to believe something
persuade	to get someone to do something

D

decent	showing acceptable behavior; moral and upright
descent	decline
dissent	disagreement
detract	to make less by taking away from
distract	to draw someone's attention from
device	a tool, gadget, or machine
devise	to create or develop

E

emigrant	a person who leaves his or her native country
immigrant	a person who settles in a new country
emigrate	to leave your native country (used with "from")
immigrate	to settle in a new country (used with "to")
envelop	to surround
envelope	a packet used to mail letters
every day	each day
everyday	ordinary

F

farther	more distant in physical space than something else (farther down the road)
further	more distant in degree or time (further along in her career)
formally	officially; properly
formerly	in the past; before this; previously

G

gap	a space between things
gape	to stare at
glance	to take a quick look
glaze	to put a shiny finish on something

H

hanged	executed someone by hanging that person by the neck
hung	put up; attached to a wall
human	a person
humane	caring; kind

I

imply	to suggest or mean
infer	to make a judgment or draw a conclusion

L

later	afterward; in a while
latter	concluding; second
lay	to place something or put something down
lie	to recline
leave	to depart
let	to allow or permit

lend	to give something to someone on a temporary basis
loan	something you give to someone on a temporary basis
lightening	making lighter
lightning	flashes of light during a thunder-storm

M

medal	a badge
metal	a hard substance
mettle	courage
moral	a lesson to be drawn, especially from a fable
morale	general way someone is feeling; confidence; spirits

O

oral	by mouth
verbal	spoken; having to do with words

P

pastor	a minister
pasture	a place where animals graze
precede	to come before in time
proceed	to carry on or continue

Challenge

A

access	entrance
assess	to evaluate or judge
adoptive	describing a parent who adopts a child (adoptive parent)
adopted	legally taken into another family (adopted child)
adverse	bad; unfavorable
averse	reluctant; against something
affective	emotional; moving
effective	causing the desired result
alleviate	to ease, lessen, or make more bearable
ameliorate	to improve
allude	to refer to indirectly
elude	to escape or avoid
allusion	an indirect reference to something
delusion	a persistent false belief; a mental disorder
illusion	a dream or fantasy; a misleading image
alternate	every other one in a series
alternative	a choice between two or more options
option	something that may be chosen

alternately	one after the other
alternatively	on the other hand
amoral	without morals; not knowing right from wrong
immoral	wicked; corrupt
appraise	to assess or evaluate
apprise	to inform or explain
assure	to promise or guarantee
ensure	to see to it that something happens or doesn't happen
insure	to guarantee protection or safety
censor	to remove offensive or problematic material
censure	an official reprimand or severe criticism
comprehensible	understandable
comprehensive	complete; covering everything
concurrent	happening at the same time
consecutive	one after the other

confidant	someone you confide in
confident	full of confidence; sure of your ability
connotation	associations brought to mind; suggested meaning
denotation	stated meaning
connote	to suggest a meaning
denote	to state a meaning
continual	occurring again and again
continuous	nonstop
currently	at this time; now
presently	in a short while; soon

D

definite	certain; exact
definitive	authoritative; final
defuse	to remove a fuse from a bomb or make a situation less tense
diffuse	spread out
dilemma	a situation involving a choice between two equally unfavorable options
predicament	any difficult and unpleasant situation

disinterested	impartial; fair
uninterested	not interested; bored

E

economic	financial
economical	thrifty; saving money
egoist	someone who is self-centered and thinks mainly of himself or herself
egotist	someone who is arrogant, very conceited, and selfish
elicit	to draw or bring out
illicit	unlawful; dishonest
eminent	well-known; famous; important
imminent	coming up; about to happen
epigram	a short, witty poem or saying
epigraph	a quotation used to set the theme for a literary work
epitaph	an inscription on a tombstone

F

flammable	able or likely to catch fire easily
inflammable	not able or likely to catch fire easily
nonflammable	not able to catch fire
flaunt	to show off
flout	to show contempt or disobey

H

historic	significant; remarkable; having an effect on history
historical	relating to the past

J

jurist	a law expert or judge
juror	a person who serves on a jury

L

luxuriant	abundant
luxurious	fond of or marked by luxury

N

nauseous	sickening; causing nausea
nauseated	feeling sick and ready to vomit

P

perfect	without flaws
prefect	a student with authority over other students
persecute	harass; treat cruelly
prosecute	to bring a case against a defendant in a trial

persecution	cruel treatment
prosecution	bringing a case against a defendant in a trial
personal	private
personnel	the people who work for a company or organization
prescribe	to recommend a treatment or course of action
proscribe	to forbid or ban

R

respectfully	in a way that shows respect
respectively	in that order

S

statue	a sculpture
stature	height or standing
statute	a law or governing rule

T

tortuous	winding; twisted
torturous	causing great pain and anguish

IRREGULAR VERBS

Most English verbs form their past-tense and past-participle forms by adding -ed to the base form or infinitive. Some verbs, though, have irregular past-tense and/or past-participle forms.

Easy

Base Form	Past Tense	Past Participle	Base Form	Past Tense	Past Participle
be	was/were	been	go	went	gone
beat	beat	beaten or beat	grow	grew	grown
become	became	become	have/has	had	had
begin	began	begun	hear	heard	heard
bend	bent	bent	hit	hit	hit
bite	bit	bitten	hold	held	held
blow	blew	blown	hurt	hurt	hurt
break	broke	broken	keep	kept	kept
bring	brought	brought	know	knew	known
build	built	built	leave	left	left
burn	burned or burnt	burned or burnt	let	let	let
buy	bought	bought	lose	lost	lost
catch	caught	caught	make	made	made
come	came	come	meet	met	met
cut	cut	cut	put	put	put
dig	dug	dug	read	read	read
do	did	done	ride	rode	ridden
drink	drank	drunk	ring	rang	rung
drive	drove	driven	run	ran	run
eat	ate	eaten	say	said	said
fall	fell	fallen	see	saw	seen
feed	fed	fed	sell	sold	sold
feel	felt	felt	send	sent	sent
fight	fought	fought	show	showed	showed or shown
find	found	found	shut	shut	shut
fly	flew	flown	sing	sang	sung
get	got	gotten	sink	sank	sunk
give	gave	given			

Base Form	Past Tense	Past Participle	Base Form	Past Tense	Past Participle
sit	sat	sat	think	thought	thought
stand	stood	stood	throw	threw	thrown
take	took	taken	wear	wore	worn
teach	taught	taught	win	won	won
tell	told	told	write	wrote	written

Target

Base Form	Past Tense	Past Participle	Base Form	Past Tense	Past Participle
arise	arose	arisen	hide	hid	hidden
awake	awoke	awoken	kneel	knelt or kneeled	knelt or kneeled
awaken	awakened	awakened	knit	knit or knitted	knit or knitted
bear	bore	born or borne	lay	laid	laid
bet	bet	bet	lead	led	led
bid	bid or bade	bidden	lend	lent	lent
bind	bound	bound	lie (recline)	lay	lain
bleed	bled	bled	mean	meant	meant
burst	burst	burst	mistake	mistook	mistaken
cast	cast	cast	misunderstand	misunderstood	misunderstood
choose	chose	chosen	overhear	overheard	overheard
cling	clung	clung	pay	paid	paid
cost	cost	cost	plead	pleaded or pled	pleaded or pled
creep	crept	crept	prove	proved	proved or proven
deal	dealt	dealt			
dream	dreamed or dreamt	dreamed or dreamt	quit	quit or quitted	quit
			redo	redid	redone
fit	fitted or fit	fitted or fit	rid	rid	rid
flee	fled	fled	rise	rose	risen
fling	flung	flung	seek	sought	sought
forbid	forbade or forbad	forbidden	shake	shook	shaken
			shed	shed	shed
forecast	forecast	forecast	shine	shone or shined	shone or shined
forget	forgot	forgotten			
freeze	froze	frozen	show	showed	shown
grind	ground	ground	shoot	shot	shot
hang (person)	hanged	hanged	shrink	shrank or shrunk	shrunk or shrunken
hang (thing)	hung	hung			

Base Form	Past Tense	Past Participle	Base Form	Past Tense	Past Participle
slay	slew	slain	strike	struck	struck or stricken
sleep	slept	slept	string	strung	strung
slide	slid	slid	swear	swore	sworn
slit	slit	slit	sweep	swept	swept
speak	spoke	spoken	swell	swelled	swollen or swelled
speed	sped or speeded	sped or speeded	swim	swam	swum
spend	spent	spent	swing	swung	swung
split	split	split	tear	tore	torn
spread	spread	spread	upset	upset	upset
spring	sprang or sprung	sprang or sprung	wake	woke or waked	woken or waked
steal	stole	stolen	weave	wove	woven
stick	stuck	stuck	weep	wept	wept
stink	stank or stunk	stank or stunk	wind	wound	wound
sting	stung	stung	wring	wrung	wrung

Challenge

Base Form	Past Tense	Past Participle	Base Form	Past Tense	Past Participle
backslide	backslid	backslid	overdo	overdid	overdone
breed	bred	bred	oversee	oversaw	overseen
broadcast	broadcast or broadcasted	broadcast or broadcasted	overtake	overtook	overtaken
			partake	partook	partaken
foresee	foresaw	foreseen	proofread	proofread	proofread
foretell	foretold	foretold	recast	recast	recast
forgive	forgave	forgiven	shear	sheared	sheared or shorn
input	inputted or input	inputted or input	typecast	typecast	typecast
miscast	miscast	miscast	undercut	undercut	undercut
mislay	mislaid	mislaid	undergo	underwent	undergone
misread	misread	misread	uphold	upheld	upheld
outbid	outbid	outbid	withdraw	withdrew	withdrawn
outgrow	outgrew	outgrown	withhold	withheld	withheld
overcome	overcame	overcome			

NOUNS WITH IRREGULAR PLURALS

Most English nouns form their plural by adding -s or -es to the singular form. Some nouns, though, have an irregular plural form. This is especially true of nouns borrowed from other languages.

Easy

Singular	Plural	Singular	Plural
child	children	mouse	mice
deer	deer	sheep	sheep
foot	feet	tooth	teeth
goose	geese	wife	wives
half	halves	wolf	wolves
man	men	woman	women

Target

Singular	Plural	Singular	Plural
antenna	antennae (or antennas)	loaf	loaves
		louse	lice
axis	axes	medium	media
basis	bases	memorandum	memoranda
bison	bison	moose	moose
bacterium	bacteria	oasis	oases
cactus	cacti (or cactuses)	octopus	octopi (or octopuses)
corps	corps	offspring	offspring
crisis	crises	ox	oxen
curriculum	curricula	person	people
datum	data	radius	radii
diagnosis	diagnoses	self	selves
die	dice	series	series
ellipsis	ellipses	shelf	shelves
hippopotamus	hippopotami (or hippopotamuses)	species	species
		swine	swine
hoofs	hooves	thief	thieves
knife	knives		
life	lives		

Challenge

Singular	Plural	Singular	Plural
alga	algae	hypothesis	hypotheses
alumna (female)	alumnae	libretto	libretti
alumnus (male)	alumni (male)	index	indices (or indexes)
amoeba	amoebae	matrix	matrices
analysis	analyses	nebula	nebulae
appendix	appendices (or appendixes)	nucleus	nuclei (or nucleuses)
		phenomenon	phenomena
chateau	chateaux	schema	schemata
criterion	criteria	stimulus	stimuli
focus	foci (or focuses)	synopsis	synopses
formula	formulae (or formulas)	synthesis	syntheses
		thesis	theses
fungus	fungi (or funguses)		

NOUNS THAT ARE ALWAYS PLURAL

Some nouns are always plural. These include words for things that always come in pairs, such as *trousers* and *pliers*, and aggregate nouns, such as *communications*, which usually end in -*s*. These words take a plural verb and/or pronoun.

Easy

clothes	mittens	shorts
jeans	pants	shoes

Target

accommodations	headquarters	shears
barracks	living quarters	sleeping quarters
binoculars	leggings	sneakers
crossroads	news	spectacles
earmuffs	overalls	sunglasses
eyeglasses	pajamas	tights
gallows	pliers	troops
gloves	police	trousers
goggles	scissors	tweezers

Challenge

archives	forceps	remains
arms	goods	(library) stacks
communications	nail clippers	tongs
contents	pinking shears	
dregs	media	

COLLECTIVE NOUNS

Collective nouns are words that name of group of people, animals, or things. When the noun refers to the group as a unit, it takes a singular verb and pronoun. When it refers to the individual members or parts of the group, it takes a plural verb and pronoun.

Collective nouns for groups of animals are also called "terms of venery." Most of them come from hunting. Some use creative or imaginative terms to describe the animals. Some can be used for people, too, such as a "congregation of birds" or a "congregation of people."

Easy

band	flock	pack
class	group	school (of fish)
family	herd	team

Target

army	colony	luggage
assembly	committee	mob
audience	company	navy
baggage	congress	nest (of mice)
batch	corporation	party
board	corps	pride (of lions)
brood (of young animals or children)	council	pod (of marine animals)
bundle	crew	set
cabinet	fleet	society
cache	gaggle (of geese)	squadron
cast	galaxy	stable (of horses)
choir	gang	streak (of tigers)
chorus	generation	swarm (of insects)
clan	horde	tribe
cluster	jury	troop
	litter	troupe

Challenge

array	exultation (of larks)	plague (of locusts)
battery	faculty	public
bevy (of larks or quail)	fraternity	sorority
brace (of wildfowl)	gam (of whales)	shoal (of fish)
cete (of badgers)	host (of angels)	shrewdness (of apes)
clowder (of cats)	kindle (of kittens)	skein (of wildfowl)
congregation	majority	skult (of vermin)
convocation (of eagles)	minority	span (of oxen)
covey (of game birds)	murder (of crows)	sloth (of bears)
drift (of hogs)	muster (of peacocks)	warren (of rabbits)
drove (of cattle or geese)	passel (of possums)	watch (of nightingales)

WORDS WITH SILENT LETTERS

Many words in English have one or more silent letters. The words below are grouped by the silent letter or letters most likely to cause problems. (This list does not include words that follow the pattern consonant-vowel-consonant-silent *e*. See p. 51).

Easy

Silent A

coat
lead
leaf
leak
lean
leap
leave
meadow
mean
meat
oak
oar
oath
soak
soap
soar

Silent B

comb
crumb
doubt
dumb
limb
tomb

Silent C

duck
fleck
jack
jacket
kick
lick
lock
locket
pack
package
pocket
rack
rock
rocket
sack
sick
sock
speck
stack
tack
ticket
thick
track
trick

Silent D

badge
budge
dodge
handsome
hedge
lodge
nudge
Wednesday

Silent E

clothe
clothes
doe
eel
eerie
ore
rinse
waste

Silent G

gnarled
gnash
gnat
gnaw
gnome
gnu

Silent GH

fight
high
light
might
right
sigh
sight
slight
tight

Silent H

cartwheel
Christmas
ghost
ghostly
pinwheel
whale
what
wheat
wheel
when
where
which
while
whip
whirl
whisker
whisper
whistle
white
why

Silent I

niece

Silent K

knack
knave
knead
knee
kneel
knife
knight
knit
knob
knock
knot
know

Silent L

half

Silent O

people

Silent R

purr

Silent T

batch
castle
catch
catcher

hatch
hitch
hitchhike
hopscotch
itch
kitchen
latch
listen
scratch
snatch
watch

Silent U

aunt
building
guard
guess
guest
guide
laugh

Silent W

sword
two
who
whole
wrap
wrist
write
writing
wrong

Target

Silent A

coarse
coax
cocoa
diamond
diaper
leaflet
league
lease
leash
leather
restaurant

Silent B

debt

Silent C

crescent
descend
descendant
discipline
jackal
jackpot
kickoff
muscle
neckerchief
necklace
padlock
racket
scene
scent
slapstick
socket
speckled

sprocket
tackle
thicket
trickle

Silent D

adjective
adjust
budget
cartridge
dislodge
dredge
edge
edgewise
fridge
gadget
grudge
hedge
porridge

Silent E

beverage
cleanse
coleslaw
collapse
commence
commerce
counterfeit
forfeit
gorgeous
horde
lacrosse
lance
lapse

lathe
legume
neutral
omelette
pageant
pasteurize
pigeon
questionnaire
rhyme
sergeant
soothe
submerge
sunbathe
surely
surge
suspense
swerve
tease
teethe
tense
thyme
value
vengeance
waste
writhe

Silent G

campaign
design
feign
foreign
lasagna

Silent GH

daughter
height
slaughter
though
through
upright
uptight

Silent H

dinghy
bushwhack
chord
choral
chorus
chronic
elsewhere
Fahrenheit
ghastly
ghetto
harpsichord
heir
heiress
heirloom
overwhelm
rhombus
rhubarb
rhyme
rhythm
shepherd
silhouette
spaghetti
vehicle
whack
wharf
wheelchair
wheeze

whether
whim
whimper
whine
whirlpool
whirlwind
whisk
whiz

Silent I

brilliant
business
peculiar

Silent K

doorknob
knapsack
knickers
knickknack
knocker
knoll
knotty
know-how
knowledge
knowledgeable
knuckle
well-known

Silent L

behalf
chalk
halve
llama
salmon

Silent N

column
condemn
hymn

Silent O

flourish
leopard
pious

Silent P

psalm
raspberry

Silent PS

corps

Silent QU

lacquer

Silent S

debris

Silent T

beret
bewitch
blotch
bouquet
bristle
butcher
butterscotch
dispatch
etch
glisten
glitch
hatchery

hatchet
hatchling
hustle
hutch
jostle
ketchup
latchkey
mistletoe
nestle
notch
often
putt
retch
rustle
sketch
snatch
stretch
switch
thatch
trestle
thistle
twitch

wrestle
wrestling
wristwatch

Silent U

biscuit
guardian
guild
guilt
guinea pig
guitar
laughable
lifeguard
mourn
safeguard
vacuum

Silent UE

catalogue
monologue
prologue
technique

Silent W

playwright
shipwreck
swordfish
wholly
whom
whooping crane
whose
wrangle
wreck
wreckage
wren
wrench
wrestle
wrestling
wretched
wriggle
wring
wrinkle
wristwatch

Silent X

Sioux

Challenge

Silent A

algae
aardvark
guinea pig
meager
pharaoh
tarpaulin

Silent B

dumbfounded

honeycomb
indebted

Silent C

abscess
czar
czarina
incandescent
obscene
scenario

scepter
sickle-cell

Silent CH

yacht

Silent D

drudgery
fledgling

Silent E

ageism
aloe
appease
coerce
entrepreneur
hieroglyphics
maneuver
neurotic
neuter
seismograph
syringe
terse
venue
verge

Silent G

align
benign
champagne
consign
consignment
phlegm

Silent GH

drought
righteous

Silent H

aghast
annihilate
Buddha
Buddhism
bushwhack
chasm
cholera
cholesterol
choral
choreographer
Christianity
chromosome
chronological
chrysalis
chrysanthemum
jodhpurs
khaki
rheumatism
rhinoceros
rhododendron
Sikh
vehement
whimsical

Silent I

parliament
plagiarize

Silent O

amoeba
colonel
jeopardy
onomatopoeia

Silent P

pneumatic
pneumonia

Silent T

apostle
chalet
debut
depot
fillet
gourmet

mortgage
ricochet
tsar
tsarina
tsunami

Silent GH

asthma
isthmus

Silent U

camouflage
cantaloupe
chauffeur
gourmet
guerrilla
guile
guillotine
quetzal

Silent UE

epilogue
queue
rogue
synagogue

Silent W

wrath
wrest
writhe

Silent X

roux

Silent Z

rendezvous

SILENT E IN C-V-C-E WORDS

Some words follow the pattern of consonant-vowel-consonant-silent e. Usually, the silent e signals that the vowel sound is long or, in multisyllabic words, the vowel sound before the last syllable is long.

Easy

1-syllable words

bake
base
bite
blade
bone
bore
cake
cane
cape
case
cave
code
crime
date
dime
dine
dive
drive
face
fine
frame
gate
gave
grace
grade
hate
hide
hole
kite
lace

lake
lame
lane
late
life
lime
live
lone
lose
love
made
mane
make
male
mate
more
name
nine
note
plane
pale
pole
rate
rise
shine
side
stole
sure
tale
tape
time
twice

twine
vase
wade
wage
wake
wave

2-syllable words

arrive
compete
complete
decide
define
describe
divide
escape
explode
explore
include
invade
ore
outside
suppose
surprise
tadpole
translate

3-syllable words

crocodile
navigate
telephone

Target

1-syllable words

bale
brace
bride
chime
choke
cite
clone
close
clove
cone
core
daze
dome
dove
fake
fare
fate
flame
fume
fuse
glaze
glide
grate
hale
hare
hose
mare
mate
pace
scene
swipe
tone
tote
truce
wage

2-syllable words

abode
abuse
alcove
arcade
astute
azure
cascade
collide
compose
comprise
concrete
console
consume
corrode
costume
cyclone
defuse
delete
deplete
depose
derive
despise
device
devote
discrete
embrace
engrave
estate
exhale
exile
expose
extreme
feline
folktale
frustrate

future
grenade
ignore
immune
impose
inflame
irate
leisure
module
outrage
reside
revise
schedule
subscribe
supreme
surname
terrace
termite
tribute
trombone
turnpike
unite
vaccine
volume
voyage

3-syllable words

absolute
aggravate
appetite
carnivore
centipede
circulate
civilize
concentrate
congregate

contemplate
dedicate
delegate
designate
dominate
emigrate
exercise
finalize
formulate
herbivore
hesitate

hibernate
homicide
illustrate
immigrate
incubate
operate
overrate
organize
paraphrase
parasite
renovate

submarine
sympathize
tangerine
undermine

4-syllable words

accommodate
domesticate
incorporate
subordinate
telecommute

Challenge

1-syllable words

bane
bode
chafe
chide
cite
clone
gale
haze
hone
jute
mete
mode
muse
name
raze
tome

2-syllable words

abate
abide
atone
estate
fissure
glucose
graphite
secrete
syndrome
turbine

3-syllable words

attribute
cellophane
cellulose
chromosome

composite
composure
germinate
gyroscope
regicide
synchronize

4-syllable words

desegregate
eradicate
espionage
gesticulate

WORDS NOT SPELLED AS THEY SOUND

There are many spelling demons in the English language, but the spelling of some words is particularly hard to fathom. Here are words that are tricky because they sound so little like they are spelled.

Easy

ache	hymn	though
acre	island	through
aisle	laugh	Tuesday
are	often	Wednesday
choir	one	weird
eighth	restaurant	why
gypsy	route	women

Target

amateur	fuel	reservoir
asthma	genius	rhyme
campaign	gymnasium	rhythm
chauffeur	hygiene	schedule
colonel	jewelry	sergeant
conscience	lacquer	subtle
conscious	lieutenant	surveillance
conscientious	mortgage	technique
corps	naughty	theater
diaphragm	nuisance	unanimous
etiquette	pageant	unique
fatigue	pamphlet	vague
faucet	penicillin	yacht
foreign	physician	
feud	pneumonia	

Challenge

archaeologist	hieroglyphics	psychiatric
archaeology	hemorrhage	psychic
archaic	isthmus	psychology
arctic	larynx	queue
champagne	lingerie	reminisce
coercion	maneuver	rendezvous
drought	pharaoh	sacrilegious
gourmet	panache	tuition
liaison	phlegm	

Chapter 2

Vocabulary Development

> **"** *I'm teaching my students how to use word parts to determine the meaning of unfamiliar words. My textbook contains some prefixes, suffixes, and roots, and I need additional ones.* **"**

One way to create new words is to add together word parts. A combining form is a word part that is combined with one or more other combining forms or a free-standing word to form a new word. Some combining forms always take the initial position. These are commonly called prefixes. Some always take the final position. These are commonly called suffixes. Some can take either position or appear in the middle of a word. These are often referred to as roots.

Another way to build new words is to add together two or more whole words. These compound words may be hyphenated (ice-cold), written with a space between the two words but treated as one entity (ice cream), or closed up with no space between the original words (airplane).

Sometimes words are shortened. A clipped word is a shortened form of a word in which the end syllables are dropped (*pop music* for *popular music*). An abbreviation is a shortened form of a word or phrase used when writing to represent the whole word (*Mr.* for *Mister*). An acronym is a word formed from the initials or other parts of several words. With an acronym, you say the word formed by the letters (*radar*, for *radio detecting and ranging*). An initialism uses only letters from the word. With an initialism, you say the letters (*CD* for *compact disc*).

PREFIXES

A prefix is a letter or group of letters added to a word or root to change its meaning.

Easy

Latin

Prefix	Meaning	How It Works	Example
non-	not; lacking; without	non + fat = nonfat; without fat	nondairy, nonfiction, nonsense, nonstick
pre-	before; in front of; superior to	pre + view = preview; look at before or ahead of time	precook, predict, preface, pretest
re-	again; back; reverse the action of	re + make = remake; make again	redo, rerun, return, review

Old English

Prefix	Meaning	How It Works	Example
mis-	bad; badly; wrongly	mis + fortune = misfortune; bad fortune	misbehave, misguided, misspelled, mistake
un-	not; the opposite of	un + fair = unfair; not fair	unable, uncover, unknown, untrue

Target

Greek

Prefix	Meaning	How It Works	Example
anti-	against; opposed to; preventing or counteracting	anti + labor = antilabor; against labor unions	antibacterial, antidote; antifreeze, antisocial
auto-	self	auto + biography = autobiography; biography; story of one's own life	autocracy, autograph, automatic, automobile, autonomous
deca-	ten	deca + gon = decagon; a ten-sided figure	decade, decameter, decathlon

Prefix	Meaning	How It Works	Example
mono-	one; alone; single	mono + tone = monotone; a single, unchanging tone	monogram, monolith, monologue, monopoly
oct-, octa-, octo-	eight	octa + gon = octagon; an eight-sided figure	octave, octet, octogenarian, octopus

Latin

Prefix	Meaning	How It Works	Example
✓ bi-	two; twice; on two sides; occurring every two; occurring twice during a period	bi + monthly = bimonthly; occurring every two months	bicycle, bilingual, bisect, biweekly
✓ co-, col-, com-, con-, cor-	together with; joint; to the same degree	con + vene = convene; to come together	copilot, collate, communication, correlate
de-	from; down; reverse the action of	de + code = decode; to reverse the action of coding; to translate a coded message	debrief, demerit, decrease, derail
✓ deci-	one-tenth	deci + mate = decimate; to destroy every tenth part	decibel, decimal, deciliter, decimeter
✓ dis-	not; opposite of; lack of; away from	dis + band = disband; to do the opposite of forming a band; to break up a band or move apart	disbelieve, discharge, disconnect, dislike
✓ equa-, equi-	equal; equally	equi + distant = equidistant; equally distant	equation, equator, equinox, equitable
em-, en-	put into or on; cover; make; subject to; intensifier	en + throne = enthrone; put on the throne; crown	embark, empower, enable, endanger
ex- (with hyphen)	former	ex- + convict = ex-convict; former convict	ex-mayor, ex-senator, ex-president, ex-wife
e-, ex-	out; beyond; away from; without	ex + pel = expel; to push out, banish, or eject	eject, emit, excavate, exceed, exclude, exhale
il-, im-, in-, ir-	not; lack of	il + legal = illegal; not legal	impartial, immature, insecure, irregular

Prefix	Meaning	How It Works	Example
im-, in-	in; into; within	in + duct = induct; lead or bring into	immerse, immigrate, inborn, income
inter-	between	inter + national = international; between nations	interact, intercoastal, intermingle, interstate
intra-	within; inside	intra + city = intracity; within a large city	intramural, intradermal, intrastate, intravenous
mal-	bad; badly; wrong; ill	mal + adjusted = maladjusted; poorly adjusted	malcontent, malady, malaise, malaria
multi	many	multi + cultural = multicultural; relating to many cultures	multilingual, multimillionaire, multiform, multiple
ob-, oc-, of-, op-	before; against; over; totally	ob + scure = obscure; cover; over	object, occur, offer, oppose
per-	through; throughout; completely; very thoroughly	per + ceive = perceive; understand or grasp thoroughly	perfect, perform, permeate, permit
post-	after; later	post + script = postscript; written afterward or at the end of a letter	posterior, posthumous, postpone, postwar
pro-	for; forward	pro + ceed = proceed; go ahead	progress, promote, pronounce, propose
sub	under; beneath; to a lesser degree, bordering	sub + ject = subject; place under someone else's authority	sublet, submerge, substandard, subway
super-, supr-	above; beyond; over	super + natural = supernatural; beyond the normal	superhighway, superscript, supersonic, supreme
trans-	across; over; beyond	trans + continental = transcontinental; crossing the continent	transact, transfer, translate, transportation
tri-	three	tri + angle = triangle, a figure with three angles	triceps, tricycle, trillion, tristate
uni-	one; only	uni + cycle = unicycle; one cycle; one wheel	uniform, unity, unique

Old English

Prefix	Meaning	How It Works	Example
by-	near; side; secondary or incidental to the main product	by + stander = bystander; person standing at the sidelines or looking on	bylaw, bypass, byproduct, byway
fore-	before; ahead of; front	fore + ground = foreground; the front or nearest part of a scene	forearm, forecast, foretell, forewarn
mid-	middle	mid + stream = midstream; the middle of the stream	midnight, midpoint, midterm, midway
over-	above; over; upper; outer; superior; passing above, beyond, or across; too much	over + weight = overweight; above normal weight	overcharge, overdue, overflow, oversee
self-	by oneself; within; automatic	self + centered = self-centered; centered on	self-confidence, selfish, self-made, self-winding
under-	beneath; too little; below normal	under + ground = underground; beneath the surface of the ground	underage, underneath, underwater, underweight

Challenge

Greek

Prefix	Meaning	How It Works	Example
acro-	high; topmost; at the extremity	acro + phobia = acrophobia; a fear of heights	acrobat, acronym, acropolis, acrostic
ambi-, amphi-	both; around; about	ambi + biguous = ambiguous; having two or more possible meanings; unclear	ambidextrous, ambivalent, amphibious, amphitheater
di-	two; double; twice	di + chromatic = dichromatic; having two colors	dichotomy, diffract, dilemma, dissect
dia-	through; throughout; apart; between	dia + lect = dialect; local language used throughout a region	diagram, diagonal, diameter, dialogue
endo-	within	endo + biotic = endobiotic; living within the body	endocardial, endocentric, endocrinology, endodermis

Prefix	Meaning	How It Works	Example
epi-	upon; over; on the outside	epi + dermis = epidermis; the outside of the skin	epicenter, epidemic, epidural, epilogue
hemi-	half	hemi + cycle = hemicycle; a half cycle	hemihedral, hemisphere, hemispheroid, hemitrope
hetero-	different	hetero + nym = heteronym; a word spelled the same as another but with a different meaning	heterochromatic, heterogeneous
hex-, hexa-	six	hexa + gon = hexagon; a figure with six sides	hexagram, hexahedral, hexameter, hexapod
homo-	same, equal to, like	homo + genize = homogenize; to make the same throughout	homochromatic, homogeneous, homograph, homonym
macro-, macr-	large; long	macro + economics = macro-economics; the field of economics dealing with all the forces at work in an economy, or the large picture	macrobiotics, macroclimate, macrocosm, macroscopic
mega-	especially large; great; powerful; mighty; one million	mega + dose = megadose; an especially large dose	megahertz, megalith, megaphone, megavitamin
meta-	change in; after; going beyond or higher; behind; between	meta + galaxy = metagalaxy; beyond or transcending a galaxy; all galaxies and all intergalactic matter	metabolize, metafiction, metamorphic, metaphor
micro-	very small; minute;	micro + biology = microbiology; the study of very small forms of life	microbe, microcomputer, microorganism, microprocessor
mono-	one; single	mono + lingual = monolingual; speaking one language	monogamy, monograph, monotone, monotonous
neo-	new; young; recent, latest	neo + logism = neologism; a new word or new meaning for a word	neoclassic, neoconservative, Neolithic, neonatal
paleo-	ancient; early	paleo + lithic = Paleolithic; relating to an early cultural period from about 2 million to 10 million B.C.	paleoanthropology, paleography, paleontology, Paleozoic
pan-	all; every; universal	pan + theon = pantheon; a temple where all gods are worshipped	pan-American, pan-Asian, pandemonium, pantheism

Prefix	Meaning	How It Works	Example
para-	at the side of; in a secondary position; beyond; characterized by	para + legal = paralegal; a person who works in a secondary position to a lawyer; an aide to a lawyer	parallel, paramedic, paranormal, parasite
penta-	five	penta + gon = pentagon; a five-sided figure	pentacle, pentagram, pentameter, pentarchy
peri-	around; about; enclosing; near	peri + scope = periscope; a tube for viewing the surrounding areas	peridontics, perimeter, peripatetic, periphery
poly-	many; much, excessive; more than	poly + chromatic = polychromatic; having more than one color	polydactyl, polygamy, polyglot, polygon
proto-	first	proto + type = prototype; the first of its kind that serves as a model	protocol, protohuman, protolithic, proton
pseudo-	false; deceptive; sham	pseudo + science = pseudoscience; a sham or false science	pseudomorph, pseudonym, pseudointellectual, pseudonymous
sest-, sex-	six	sest + et = sestet; poem of six lines	sestina, sexagenarian, sextet, sextuple
syl-, sym-, syn-, sys-	with; together	syn + chronize = synchronize; to happen at the same time	syllable, sympathy, synonym, system
tele-	far away; at, over, or from a distance	tele + scope = telescope; a device for seeing things far away	telegenic, telephone, teleport, televise

Latin

Prefix	Meaning	How It Works	Example
ab-, abs-	from; away	ab + duct = abduct; lead or take away; kidnap	abdicate, abject, absolve, absorb
√ ante-	before; in front of; prior to	ante + bellum = antebellum; before the war, particularly the Civil War	anteroom, antecedent, antedate, antemeridian
√ bene-	good; well	bene + factor = benefactor; a person who does good for another; patron	benediction, beneficiary, benefit, benevolent
circum-	around; about; on all sides	circum + scribe = circumscribe; to draw to line around; to limit	circumference, circumnavigate, circumstance, circumvent

Prefix	Meaning	How It Works	Example
contra-, contro-	against; opposed to; opposite of	contra + dict = contradict; say the opposite of	contraband, contradiction, contrary, controversy
counter-	against; opposite of	counter + attack = counterattack; attack a force that has attacked you	counteract, counterfit, counterclockwise, counterproductive
demi-, semi-	half; less than usual	semi + circle = semicircle; half circle	demigod, demitasse, semiannual, semiformal
extra-, extr-, extro-	outside; beyond	extra + curricular = extracurricular; beyond or outside normal curriculum	extraordinary, extravagant, extremity, extrovert
infra-	beneath; below	infra + sonic = infrasonic; below the audible range of sound	infrared, infrahuman, infrastructure
medi-, medio-	middle; half; between	medi + eval = medieval; referring to the Middle Ages	median, mediate, medium, mediocre
omni-	all; everywhere	omni + potent = omnipotent; all powerful	omnidirectional, omnipresent, omniscient, omnivore
retro-	backward; back; contrary to; behind	retro + active = retroactive; to make active or apply to an earlier or back period	retrofit, retrograde, retrospective, retroversion
ultra-	beyond; more than; excessive	ultra + sonic = ultrasonic; above the range of sound that can be heard by the human ear	ultraconservative, ultramodern, ultranationalism, ultraviolet

Old English

Prefix	Meaning	How It Works	Example
a-, an-	not; without	a + moral = amoral; without morals	anarchy, apathy, atypical, atonal

SUFFIXES

A suffix is a letter or group of letters added to the end of a word or root to form a new word and usually to change the part of speech. Adding a suffix often involves some spelling change to the base word.

Easy

Old English

Prefix	Forms	Meaning	How It Works	Examples
-ar, -er, -or	a noun	someone who; something that; native of	act + or = actor; someone who acts	baker, New Yorker, sailor, scholar
-er	a comparative adjective or adverb	more than (comparing two things)	kind + er = more kind than	colder, quicker, taller, wiser
-est	a superlative adjective or adverb	most (compares three or more things)	kind + est = kindest, the most kind	fastest, loudest, shortest, smartest
-ful	an adjective	full of; having the quality of; able to cause	harm + ful = harmful; able to cause harm	beautiful, careful, doubtful, pitiful
-less	an adjective	without; not able to be	color + less = colorless; without color	countless, soundless, spotless, weightless
-ly	an adverb or adjective	in the manner of; in the order of; every; like; having the characteristics of	year + ly = yearly; happening every year	daily, neatly, quickly, slowly
-ness	a noun	state of; quality of	good + ness = goodness; quality of being good	happiness, kindness, newness, soundness

Target

Greek

Prefix	Forms	Meaning	How It Works	Examples
-ic	an adjective	having the characteristics of; causing	hero + ic = heroic; having the qualities of a hero	alphabetic, horrific, numeric, scientific

Prefix	Forms	Meaning	How It Works	Examples
-ish	an adjective or noun	having characteristics of; somewhat native of	gray + ish = grayish; somewhat gray	childish, reddish, selfish, Swedish
-ist	a noun	a person who; that which	piano + ist = pianist; person who plays the piano	artist, dentist, extremist, specialist
-meter	a noun	device for measuring; measure	thermo + meter = thermometer; device for measuring temperature	barometer, diameter, pentameter, perimeter
-scope	a noun	an instrument for seeing	tele + scope = telescope; instrument for seeing distances	microscope, kaleidoscope, periscope, stethoscope

Latin

Prefix	Forms	Meaning	How It Works	Examples
-able -ible	an adjective	capable of; likely to; worthy of; that can or will	do + able = able; that can be done	enjoyable, laughable, likeable, sensible
-al, -ial	an adjective or a noun	of; related to; having the characteristics of; the process of	person + al = personal; related to a person; private	manual, nocturnal, reversal, seasonal
-ant, -ent	a noun or adjective	someone who; agent of; performing the tasks of; having the qualities of	depend + ent = dependent; someone who depends on other	attendant, defiant, resistant, superintendent
-ation, -ion, -sion, -tion	a noun	act of; state of; process of	communicate + ion = communication; act of communicating	action, appreciation, division, revision
-cian, -ian	a noun	a person who practices or performs a skill or art	magic + ian = magician; person who performs magic	dietician, mathematician, musician, physician
-ese	a noun or adjective	native of; language of	China + ese = Chinese; language of China	Burmese, Cantonese, Japanese, Portuguese, Vietnamese
-fy	a verb	make	beauty + fy = beautify; make beautiful	clarify, justify, magnify, simplify

Prefix	Forms	Meaning	How It Works	Examples
-ile	an adjective	related to; capable of; suitable for	mob + ile = mobile; capable of moving	docile, juvenile, puerile, senile
-ity, -ty	a noun	state of; quality of being; instance of	creative + ity = creativity; state of being creative	ability, loyalty, nationality, possibility
-ive, -ative, -itive	an adjective	causing; tending to do something; having the quality of	sense + itive = sensitive; tending to sense or feel things strongly	conservative, creative, destructive, instructive
-ment	a noun	action of; process of; result of; degree of being	enchant + ment = enchantment; action or or state of feeling enchanted	achievement, enjoyment, government, retirement
-ous, -eous, -ious	an adjective	full of; having the qualities of	joy + ous = joyous; full of joy	generous, glorious, mysterious, nervous

Old English

Prefix	Forms	Meaning	How It Works	Examples
-en	an adjective	made of; added to	wax + en = made of wax	flaxen, silken, wooden, woolen
-hood	a noun	place; time; period; state of; quality of; group of	boy + hood = boyhood; period when one is a young boy	adulthood, childhood, neighborhood, priesthood
-like	an adjective	similar to; resembling	home + like = homelike; resembling home	childlike, deathlike, dreamlike, lifelike
-ship	a noun	condition of; state of; quality of being; art or skill of	hard + ship = hardship; condition of being hard; difficulty	authorship, dicta-torship, friendship, leadership
-ward	an adjective or adverb	in the direction of	down + ward = downward; in the direction of down	backward, homeward, onward, upward
-y	an adjective	characterized by; inclined to; tending to; somewhat	stick + y = sticky; tending to stick	curly, dirty, happy, itchy

Challenge

Greek

Prefix	Forms	Meaning	How It Works	Examples
-asis, -esis, -osis	a noun	action; condition; process	hypno + osis = hypnosis; condition of being hypnotized	stasis, hypothesis, synthesis, thesis
-cy	a noun	action; function; rank; condition or fact of being	bankrupt + cy = bankruptcy; condition of being bankrupt	delicacy, democracy, papacy, supremacy
-ism	a noun	act of; state of; system; manner; school of	terror + ism = terrorism; act of creating terror	communism, cubism, heroism, pluralism
-itis	a noun	disease; inflammation of; excessive preoccupation with	tonsil + itis = tonsillitis; inflammation of the tonsils	arthritis, bronchitis, laryngitis, neuritis
-ize	a verb	make; cause to become; subject to; engage in	theory + ize = theorize; engage in forming theories	generalize, sanitize, penalize, verbalize
-mania	a noun	exaggerated enthusiasm; madness; uncontrollable desire	pyro + mania = pyromania; uncontrollable desire to, set fire to things	balletomania, egomania kleptomania, megalomania
-ology; -logy	a noun	study of; science of; branch of learning	bio + logy = biology; study of all forms of life	archeology, astronomy, physiology, psychology
-phobia	a noun	fear; hatred	arachno + phobia = arachnophobia; fear of spiders	acrophobia, claustrophobia, hydro phobia, necrophobia

Latin

Prefix	Forms	Meaning	How It Works	Examples
-ance, -ancy	a noun	state of; quality of; act of; process of	rely + ance = reliance; state of relying	appearance, defiance, hesitancy, truancy
-ary, -ory	a noun or adjective	relating to; having the qualities of; place where or for	sense + ory = sensory; relating to the senses	dictionary, dormitory, sanctuary, secondary

Prefix	Forms	Meaning	How It Works	Examples
-ate	a verb	cause; make; provide or treat with	vaccine + ate = vaccinate; provided with or treated with a vaccine	calculate, evaluate, notate, validate
-cide	a noun	kill; killing; killer	fratri + cide = fratricide; killing one's brother	herbicide, homicide, pesticide, suicide
-ence, -ency	a noun	state of; quality	depend + ence = dependence; state of depending on others	absence, evidence, independence transparency
-ery	a noun	place to or for; practice of; product of; collection of; condition of	green + ery = greenery; collection of plants	brewery, eatery, robbery, scenery
-ice	a noun	condition of; state of	coward + ice = cowardice; state of being cowardly	avarice, jaundice, justice, malice
-tude	a noun	state of; condition of; instance of being	magni + tude = magnitude; condition of being important or of great size	altitude, gratitude, multitude, platitude
-ure	a noun	state of being; process of; condition of; result of; office of; collected body of	seize + ure = seizure; state of being seized	censure, culture, legislature, literature

Old English

Prefix	Forms	Meaning	How It Works	Examples
-dom	a noun	quality of; state of; realm of; power of	king + dom = kingdom; realm of the king	boredom, freedom, serfdom, wisdom

Old French

Prefix	Forms	Meaning	How It Works	Examples
-ee	a noun	one who is receiving the action or performing the action	employ + ee = employee; person who is employed	evacuee, referee, refugee, trainee

ROOTS

A word root is the basic meaningful part of a word from which other words are built. A root cannot stand alone as a word but needs a prefix and/or suffix added to it.

Easy

Greek

Root	Meaning	How It Works	Example
graph	written; drawn; recorded	graph + ic + s = graphics; drawings	autograph, biography, geography, graphically, photography

Latin

Root	Meaning	How It Works	Example
dic, dict	speak; say; tell	pre + dict + ion = prediction; the act of foretelling; forecast	dictator, dictionary, indicate, verdict
ject	throw; cast	re + ject + ion = rejection; being cast out or thrown out	dejected, injection, project, reject
port	carry	trans + port + ation = transportation the carrying of goods and people across distances	deport, portable, reporter, teleport

Target

Greek

Root	Meaning	How It Works	Example
bio	life; of living things	micro + bio + logy = microbiology; study of very tiny living things	autobiography, biography, biology, bioengineering, biofeedback
chron, chrono	time	syn + chron + ize = synchronize; make the same time	chronic, chronology, chronological, chronometer
gen	birth; race; product of	gen + erate = generate; give birth to or create	generation, generic, homogeneous, progeny
geo	earth	geo + logy = geology; study of the earth	geochemistry, geography, geode, geologist

Root	Meaning	How It Works	Example
gram	written; letter; recorded	mono + gram = monogram; one or more letters standing for a name	electrocardiogram, grammar, grammatical, telegram
path, pass	disease; suffering; feeling	sym + path + etic = identifying with with someone else's suffering	compassion, empathy, passionate, pathology
phil	love	phil + osophy = philosophy; love of learning	bibliophile, Francophile, philanthropist, philosopher
phon, phono	sound	tele + phone = telephone; a device for carrying the sound of the human voice over distances	microphone, phoneme, phonetic, symphony
photo	of or produced by light	photo + graph = photograph; a picture taken with light	photocopy, photoengraving, photokinesis, telephoto
sci	know	omni + sci + ent = omniscient; all knowing	conscientious, conscious, pseudoscience, scientific
therm	heat	hypo + therm + ia = hypothermia; very low body temperature	thermal, thermodynamics, thermometer, thermos

Latin

Root	Meaning	How It Works	Example
alter	other	alter + ate = alternate; every other one	alter ego, alternative, alternator, unalterable
anni, annu, enni	year	semi + annu + al = semiannual; happening every	anniversary, annuity, biannual, centennial half year
aqua, aque	water	aqua + rium = aquarium; tank filled with water for fish	aquaplane, aquamarine, aqueduct, subaquatic
aud, audi	hear, hearing	aud + ible = audible; able to be heard	audience, auditor, auditorium, inaudible
cap, capt, ceive, cept	take; seize	capt + ure = capture; seize	captivate, deceive, intercept, receive
capit, capt	head; principal, most important	capit + al = capital; the head or seat of government	captain, capitalize, decapitation

Root	Meaning	How It Works	Example
cede, ceed, ced, cess	move; yield; give up	re + cede = recede; move away; withdraw	cessation, depression, recess, succession
civ	public; citizen	civ + ic = civic; relating to citizens	civil, civilian, civilization, uncivil
clam, claim	shout; cry out	ex + clam + ation = exclamation; something shouted out	clamor, proclaim, reclaim
clud, cluse	shut	re + clus + ive = reclusive; shutting yourself off from others	conclusion, exclusive, include, seclude
cred	believe; belief	cred + ible = credible; believable	credit, credulous, incredible, incredulous
cur, curs	run	re + cur + sive = recursive; running again and again; repeating itself	concurrent, cursive, cursory, precursor
derm	skin	epi + derm + is = epidermis; the outer part of the skin	dermatology, hypodermic, pachyderm, taxidermist
doc	lead	doc + ile = docile; easily taught or lead	doctor, doctrine, documentary, indoctrinate
dorm	sleep	dorm + itory = dormitory; place where a group of people sleep	dormant, dormancy, dormouse, nondormant
duc, duct	lead	aque + duct = aqueduct; a pathway for leading water	educate, induct, reduce, viaduct
fac, fact, fec, fic	make; do	fact + ory = factory; a place where things are made	facsimile, fictional, infect, manufacture
fer	carry; bear	trans + fer = transfer; carry across; move, or relocate	ferry, inference, refer, referee
flect, flex	bend	re + flect = reflect; bend back or reproduce an image	deflect, flexibility, inflexible, reflection
form	shape	re + form = reform; form again or change for the better	deform, information, reformatory, uniform
fract, frag	break	fract + ure = fracture; a break, split, or crack	fragile, fragment, infraction, refract
hab, habit	live; have, hold	in + hab + it = inhabit; live in	habitant, habitat, habitation, inhabitable

Root	Meaning	How It Works	Example
junct	join	junct + ion = junction; the point where two things meet or join	adjunct, conjunction, disjunctive, injunction
jud, judi, judic, jur, juris	aw	judic + ial = judicial; relating to the law	judiciary, jurist, juror, prejudicial
lab	work	col + lab +orate = collaborate; work together	collaboration, elaboration, laboratory, laborious
leg, legis	law	legis + lature = legislature; place where laws are made	illegal, legal, legitimate, illegitimate
liber	free	liber + ate = liberate; make free	liberal, liberation, liberalize, liberty
loc, loco	place	loc + ation = location; place	dislocate, localize, locate, relocation
magn, magni	large; great	magni + fy = magnify; make larger	magnanimous, magnification, magnificent, magnitude
man, manu	hand	manu + al = manual; done by hand	emancipate, manicure, manufacture, manuscript
mand	order	counter + mand = countermand; give an order that makes invalid a previous order	commander, demand, mandate, reprimand
mar, mari, mer	sea	sub + mar + ine = submarine; a ship that goes under the sea	aquamarine, marina, mariner, mermaid
mem	mind	re + mem + brance = remembrance; bringing to mind; honoring memory	commemorate, memorandum, memorialize,
migr, migra	wander; move; change	im + migr + ate = immigrate; move to another country	emigrant; immigration, migration, migratory
miss, mit	send	trans + miss + ion = transmission; send across space; broadcast	admission, emit, missile, omission
mob, mot, mov	move	im + mob + ile = immobile; not movable; motionless	automobile, emotion, mobility, removable
nat	to be born; birth	un + nat + ural = unnatural; not arising from nature or birth	native; nativity, preternatural, supernatural
nomen, nomin	name	nomin + ate = nominate; name someone for order	cognomen, nomenclature, nominee, nominal

Root	Meaning	How It Works	Example
nov	new	novel + ty = novelty; something new and different	innovate, nova, novel, renovation
numer	number	numer + ical = numerical; using numbers	enumerate, enumerable, numerator, numerous
pac	peace	pac + ify = pacify; make peaceful	pacific, pacifier, pacifist, pacifism
ped, pod	foot	ped + estrian = pedestrian; someone who gets from place to place on foot	centipede, pedestal, octopod, podiatrist
pel, puls	drive; urge	re + pel = repel; drive back	compulsion, expel, impulse, propulsion
pend, pens	hang, weigh	sus + pens + ion = suspension; supporting framework for something that hangs, such as a bridge	dispense, expend, pendulum, impending
pon, pos	put, place	post + pone + ment = postponement; placed at a later date; delayed	component, deposit, opposition, posture
pop	people	un + pop + ulated = unpopulated; not filled with people	depopulate, populace, popularity, unpopular
port	carry	trans + port = transport; carry across a distance	deportation, export, import, portage
put	think; suppose; estimate; reckon; consider	com + put + ation = computation; calculation or final reckoning	computer, dispute, reputation, repute
quer, ques, quir, quis	ask	in + quir + y = inquiry; questions about; formal investigation	inquisitive, query, quest, question
rupt	break, tear	inter + rupt = interrupt; break into a conversation	corrupt, disruption, erupt, rupture
scrib, script	write	pre + script + ion = prescription; written request or order for medication	conscript, describe, inscription, scribble
sign, signi	mark; indication	sign + al = signal; a mark or indication to do something	consignment, insignia, resignation, significant

Root	Meaning	How It Works	Example
spec, spect	look	in + spect + ion = inspection; a formal look or investigation of something	introspective, perspective, spectacles, spectator
sphere	ball; sphere	hemi + sphere = hemisphere; half sphere	atmosphere, spherical, spheroid, stratosphere
spir	breath; courage	re + spir + ation = respiration; breathing in and out	aspire, inspiration, perspiration, spiritual
spond, spons	answer	re + spons + ible = responsible; being answerable for something	correspond, despondent, irresponsible, sponsor
stru, struct	build; arrange	de + struct + ion = destruction; act of tearing down what was built or arranged	construction, instruct, instructure, structure
tact, tang	touch	tang + ible = tangible; able to be touched	contact, intact, tactile, intangible
terr, terra	earth; land	extra + terr + estrial = extraterrestrial; beyond the earth	terra cotta, territorial, terrace, terrarium
tract	pull; drag	re + tract + ion = retraction; something pulled or taken back	attractive, contract, detract, subtract
vac	empty	e + vac + uate = evacuate; empty of people; leave	vacancy, vacate, vacuous, vacuum
vid, vis	see	e + vid + ence = evidence; proof that that allows a person's guilt to be seen	envision, revise, television, videocassette

Challenge

Greek

Root	Meaning	How It Works	Example
anthr, anthro, anthrop	man	phil + anthrop + ist = philanthropist; person who gives money away to help humankind	anthropology, anthropomorphic misanthropic, philanthropy
arch	chief, first, ruler	mon + arch + y = monarchy; government with one ruler, usually a king or queen	archbishop, archeology, matriarch, patriarch

Root	Meaning	How It Works	Example
aster, astr	star	astro + nomy = astronomy; study of stars and star systems	asteroid, astrologist, astronaut, disaster
bibl, bibli, biblio	book	biblio + graphy = bibliography; list of books and other works consulted	biblical, bibliographer, bibliomania, bibliophile
chrom, chromo	color	mono + chrom + atic = monochromatic; having one color	chromosphere, chromosome, monochrome, polychromatic
cosm	universe; world	micro + cosm = microcosm; a miniature	cosmic, cosmonaut, cosmopolitan, macrocosm
cycl, cyclo	ring; circle; wheel	bi + cycle = bicycle; a machine with two wheels	cyclical, cyclone, recycle, tricycle
dem, demo	people	demo + cracy = democracy; government by the people	demography, epidemic, pandemic
dox	belief, opinion; praise	para + dox = paradox; two seemingly contradictory opinions or beliefs	doxology, heterodoxy, orthodox, orthodoxy
dyna, dynam, dynamo	strength; power	dynam + ic = dynamic; showing force and power; full of energy	aerodynamic, dynamite, dynamo, hydrodynamics
gam	marriage	mono + gam + y; one marriage	bigamist, bigamy, polygamist, polygamy
gnos	know	dia + gnos + is = diagnosis; knowing the cause of a disease	agnostic, diagnostician, Gnostic, prognosis
helio	sun	helio + trope = heliotrope; a plant that turns to the sun	heliocentric, heliograph, heliostat, heliotherapy
hemo	blood	hemo + stat = hemostat; something used to stop bleeding	hemoglobin, hemophilia, hemorrhage, hemotoxin
hydr, hydra, hydro	water	hydro + phobia = hydrophobia; fear of water	dehydrated, hydrodynamics, hydroelectricity, hydrothermal
lex	word; speech	lexi + con = lexicon; special words used in a field of study	alexia, dyslexic, lexical, lexicographer
lith	stone	mono + lith = monolith; one large stone standing by itself	lithography, lithosphere, megalith, neolithic

Root	Meaning	How It Works	Example
log, logue	word; speaking	mono + logue= monologue; speech by one person	catalog, dialogue, epilogue, logical
morph	shape	a + morph + ous = amorphous; having no set shape	anthropomorphic, metamorphosis, morphology, polymorph
onym	name	an + onym + ous = anonymous; without a name; unsigned or unidentified	acronym, antonym, pseudonym, synonymous
ortho	straight; upright; correct	un + ortho + dox = not conforming to correct or proper beliefs	orthodontics, orthography, orthopedics, orthotics
poli	city; state	metro + poli + tan = metropolitan; referring to a large urban area, usually including a city and its suburbs	cosmopolitan, police, policy, politician
psych, psycho	mind; spirit	psycho + logy = psychology; the science of the human mind and mental states	psychic, psychoanalysis, psychopath, psychotherapy
soph	wise	soph + omore = sophomore; "wise fool"; a second-year student	philosophy, philosopher, sophisticated, sophomoric
tox	poison	tox + ic = toxic; poisonous	antitoxin, intoxication, toxicology, toxin

Latin

Root	Meaning	How It Works	Example
agr, agri, agro	field	agri + culture = agriculture; science or field of farming	agrarian, agribusiness, agrochemical, agronomy
anim	life, spirit	anim + ate = animate; make lively; give life to	animal, inanimate, magnanimous, reanimate
belli	war	belli + cose = bellicose; given to warlike or aggressive behavior	antebellum, belligerent, rebel, rebellion
brei, brev, brevi	short	ab + brevi + ate = abbreviate; shorten	abbreviation, brief, breviary, brevity

Root	Meaning	How It Works	Example
card, cardio, cord, cor	heart	cardio + logy = cardiology; field of medicine specializing in the heart	cardiac, cordial, electro-cardiogram, encourage
carn, carni	flesh	carni + vore = carnivore; flesh-eating mammal	carnage, carnival, carnivorous, reincarnation
centr, centri, contro	central; center	con + centr + ic = concentric; with the same center or midpoint	centrifugal, centrist, eccentric, egocentric
cogn	know	re + cogn + ize = recognize; know again; identify	cognition, cognomen, incognito, recognition
corp	body	in + corp + orate = incorporate; legally form an organization	corpulent, corporeal, corpse, corpus
cura, cure	care	mani + cure = manicure; treatment to care for hands and nails	curative, curator, pedicure, incurable
den, dent, dont	tooth	dent + al = dental; relating to the teeth	dentist, dentures, orthodontist, periodontal
domin	master	domin + ate = dominate; master or subdue someone or something; control	domineer, dominion, indomitable, predominate
don, donat	give	donat + ion = donation; a gift	donor, condone, donate, pardon
fid, feder	faith; trust	con + fid + ence = confidence; faith in yourself	bona fide, federation, fidelity, infidel
fin	end; final; limit	fin + ish = finish; end	define, final, finite, infinite
frater, fratri	brother	frater + nity = fraternity; a society of men who act like brothers	confraternity, fraternal, fratricide, fraternize
grat	pleasing; favor; oblige	grat + itude = gratitude; the state of feeling pleased; appreciation	gratis, gratuitous, gratuity, ingratitude
luc, lum, lumin	light	il + lumin + ate = illuminate; shed light on	lucid, luminescence, luminous, translucent
mater, matri	mother	mater + nal = maternal; showing the characteristics of a mother	maternity, matrimony, matriarch, matriarchy
mon	advise; warn	pre + mon + ition = premonition; warning about a future event	admonish, admonishment, monitor, monument

Root	Meaning	How It Works	Example
mor, mori, mort	death	im + mort + al = immortal; not able to die; lasting forever	immortality, morbid, moribund, mortality
mut	change	im + mut + able = immutable; not able to be changed	commute, mutant, mutate, mutation
pater, patri-	father	patri + ot = patriot; a person loyal to the fatherland or homeland	paternal, patricide, repatriate, unpatriotic
reg, regi	rule, guide, straight	regi + cide = regicide; killing of the ruler	regal, regent, regime, regiment
sacr, secr	holy; secret	sacri + lege = sacrilege; violating something considered holy	consecrate, desecrate, sacrifice, sacred
sens, sent	feel	con + sens + us = consensus; joint feeling or opinion	consent, resentment, sensory, sentiment
somn	sleep	in + somn + ia = insomnia; inability to sleep	insomniac, somnambulate, somnambulist, somnolent
soror	sister	soror + ity = sorority; a group of women who act like sisters	sororal, sororate, sororicide,
tempo	ime	con + tempo + rary = contemporary; living at the same time	extemporary, tempo, temporize, temporary
ten, tens	pull; stretch	ex + tens + ion = extension; expansion or addition	extend, pretend, tension, tenuous
tort, tors	twist	con + tort + ion = contortion; twisting of the body	distort, retort, torsion, torture
ven, vent	meet	con + vent + ion = convention; meeting of a large group of people	advent, event, invention, venture
vert, vers	turn	re + vers + al = reversal; turning around or back	advertise, convert, extrovert, version
vict, vinc	conquer	con + vict + ion = conviction; finding someone guilty; conquering doubts about a person's innocence	convince, evict, invincible, victory
vig, vit, viv	life	viv + id = vivid; lively	vigorous, vitamin, vivacious, vivisection

COMPOUND WORDS

A compound word consists of two or more words joined together to form a new word. Compound words can be closed up with no space between the two original words, hyphenated, or written with a space between the original words.

Easy

Amount

every
everybody
everyday
everyone
everything
everywhere

no
nobody

no one
nothing
nowhere

some
somebody
someday
somehow
someone

someplace
something
sometime
sometimes
somewhat
somewhere

Animals

bird
birdbath
birdcage
birdcall
birddog
bird feed
birdhouse
birdseed
birdshot
bird's nest
bird watcher
bluebird
redbird
snowbird

cat
catbird

catbird seat
cat burglar
catcall
catfight
catfish
catgut
catnap
cat's cradle
cat's-eye
cat's paw
cattail

dog
dog biscuit
dogcart
dog collar
dog days

dog ear
dogfight
dogfish
doggie bag
doghouse
dog paddle
dogsled
dog tag
hangdog
seeing-eye dog
watchdog

Home and Furniture

bath
bathmat
bathrobe
bathroom
bathtub
bathwater

bed
bedbug
bedchamber
bedclothes
bedcover
bedpost
bedroll
bedroom
bedside
bedsitter
bedsore
bedspread
bedspring
bedtime

chair
armchair
side chair

clock
alarm clock
clock radio
clock-watching
clockwork
digital clock
grandfather clock

door
backdoor
doorbell
doorknob
doorstep
doorstop
doorway
front door

floor
floorboard
floor cloth
floor lamp
floor plan

room
bathroom
bedroom

dining room
living room

table
coffee table
end table
side table
tablecloth
table linen
tablespoon
table lamp
tabletop
tableware

wall
wall hanging
wallpaper
wall plug
wall-to-wall

window
window box
windowpane
window seat
window shade
windowsill

People and Family Relationships

baby
baby boom
baby boomer
baby carriage
baby grand
babysit
babysitter
baby tooth

brother
brother-in-law
stepbrother

child
childbirth
child care
child labor
childproof
child's play

father
father-in-law
fatherland
grandfather
grandfather clock
great-grandfather
stepfather

folk

folk dance

folklore

folk music

folksinger

folk song

folktale

man

manhandle

manhole

manhunt

manpower

menfolk

men's wear

men's room

mother

grandmother

great-grandmother

motherboard

mother hen

mother-in-law

motherland

motherlode

stepmother

parent

grandparent

great-grandparent

stepparent

sister

sister-in-law

stepsister

teen

teenage

teenager

woman

womanpower

women's movement

women's rights

women's room

women's wear

Time

day

day bed

daybreak

daycare

daydream

day job

day labor

daylight

daylily

daylong

daypack

dayroom

day school

day shift

daytime

day-tripper

daywear

night

night blindness

nightclothes

nightgown

nightlight

nightlong

night owl

night school

night shift

night shirt

nightstand

night table

nighttime

night watch

nightwear

spring

spring break

spring-cleaning

spring fever

springtime

summer

summerhouse

summer school

summertime

winter

winter break

wintergreen

winterkill

wintertime

Transportation

boat
boathouse
boat people
boat train
motorboat
rowboat
sailboat

bus
bus driver
busload
bus stop

car
carfare
carjack
car phone
carpool
carport
car seat
car sick
car wash
railcar
sidecar
sports car

plane
airplane
biplane
monoplane
seaplane

truck
truck driver
truck farm
truckload
truck stop

Target

Celestial Words

moon
moonbeam
moon blindness
moon-faced
moonlight
moonquake
moonrise
moonscape
moonstone
moonstruck
moonwalk

lunar
lunar month
lunarscape
lunar year

star
starburst
star-crossed

stardust
starfish
starfish flower
star fruit
stargazer
starlight
starry-eyed

solar
solar battery
solar cell
solar day
solar flare
solar heating
solar house
solar month
solar panel
solar system
solar power

solar wind
solar year

sun
sunbeam
sunblock
sunburn
sunburst
sundial
sundown
sun porch
sunrise
sunscreen
sunset
sunshade
sunshine
sunspot

Colors

black
blackball
black bear
blackberry
blackbird
blackboard
black cherry
black eye
black-eyed pea
black-eyed Susan
blackfish
black hole
blacklist
blackmail
black market
blackout
blacksmith
blacktop
black widow

blue
bluebell
blueberry
bluebird
bluebonnet
blue cheese
blue chip
blue-collar
bluefish
bluegrass
blue jeans

blue moon
blueprint
blue ribbon
bluestone

green
greenbelt
green card
greengrocer
greenhouse
green light
greens keeper
green tea

orange
orangeade
orange juice
orange stick
orangewood

red
redbird
red blood cell
red-blooded
redbreast
red carpet
redfish
red flag
red-handed
redhead
red herring
red-hot

red-letter
red maple

white
white birch
white blood cell
white bread
whitecap
white chocolate
white-collar
whitefish
white flag
white heat
white-hot
white knight
whiteout
white noise
white pages
white paper
white space
white tie
whitewash
white water

yellow
yellowbird
yellow fever
yellowfin tuna
yellow jacket
yellow journalism
yellow pages

Food

bread
breadbasket
breadboard
breadbox
breadline
bread pudding
breadstuff
breadwinner
rye bread
white bread

cheese
cheeseburger
cheesecake
cheesecloth
grilled cheese

chicken
chicken breast
chicken feed
chicken-fried
chicken run
chicken wire

fish
fishcake
fish farm
fish fry
fish head
fishhook
fishing rod
fishnet
fishpond
fish stick
fishtail

food
food poisoning
food processor
food pyramid
food service
food stamps
foodstuff
food web

meat
meatball
meatloaf
meat market

milk
ice milk
milk shake
milk toast
malted milk

Human Body

arm
armband
armchair
armhole
armrest

blood
blood bank
blood donor
bloodhound
bloodshed
bloodshot
bloodstream
bloodthirsty
blood vessel
cold-blooded

hot-blooded
warm-blooded

brain
brainchild
brainstorm
brainwash

brow
browbeat
eyebrow
highbrow
lowbrow

ear
earache
eardrum

earmuffs
earring

eye
eyeball
eye bank
eyebrow
eye-catching
eye chart
eyedropper
eyeglasses
eyehole
eyelash
eyelid
eye opener
eyeshade

eyesight
eyestrain
eyewitness
starry-eyed

face
barefaced
face cloth
face-off
faceplate
face-saver
face-to-face

finger
finger hole
fingernail
finger-paint
fingerpick
fingerprint
fingertip

foot
barefoot
football
footbath
foot bridge
foot fault
foot gear
foothill
foothold
footlights
footlocker
footloose
footpad
footpath
footprint
footrace
foot soldier
footsore
footstep
footstool

footwear
footwork

hand
backhand
handbag
handball
handbill
handbrake
handcar
handcart
handclasp
handcuff
hand-me-down
handpick
handsaw
handshake
handspring
handstand
hand-woven
handwriting

head
headache
headband
headboard
head cold
headcount
headdress
headfirst
headgear
headlamp
headlight
headline
headmaster
headphone
headpiece
headrest
headroom
headscarf
headshake

headshot
headstand
head-to-head

heart
downhearted
heartache
heart attack
heartbeat
heartbreak
heartburn
heart disease
heart failure
heartfelt
heart rate
heartsick
heartstring
heartwarming

nose
noseband
nosebleed
nosedive
nosepiece
nose-ring

toe
toecap
toe dance
toehold
toenail
toe shoe

waist
waistband
waistcoat
waistline
waist pack

wrist
wristband
wristwatch

Position

down

down-and-out
downbeat
downcast
downdraft
downfallen
downfield
downgrade
downhearted
down-home
downlink
download
down payment
downplay
downright
downriver
downscale
downshift
downside
downsize
downspin
downstage
downstairs
downstream
downswing
down-to-earth
downtown
downturn
downwind

up

up-and-coming
upbeat
up-close
update
updraft
upend

upfront
upgrade
uphill
upland
uplift
uplink
upload
upraise
uprising
upriver
upside
upstage
upstairs
up-tempo
upturn
upwind

center

center back
center field
center fielder
centerfold
centerline
center of gravity
centerpiece
center spread
center stage

side

countryside
flipside
sideband
sidebar
sideboard
sidecar
side chair
side dish
side effect

sidekick
sideline
sideslip
sidestep
sidestroke
sideswipe
sidetrack
sideways

high

high beam
highbrow
highchair
high country
high-end
high-flying
high frequency
high-grade
high ground
high-handed
high horse
highlander
highlands
highlight
high profile
high-rise
high-risk
high road
high school
high seas
high-strung
highway
high wire

low

low beam
lowbrow
low country

low-end
low-frequency
low-grade
low ground
lowland
low profile
low-rise
low-risk
low road

in
indoors
inland
inroad
inside

out
outbuilding
outdoors
outhouse
outland
outpost
outside

front
front-end
frontline
front list
frontmatter
front office
frontrunner
front yard
waterfront

back
backache
backbone
back country
backdate
backdoor

backdrop
back-end
backfield
backfire
backflip
background
backhand
backlash
backlist
backlog
backmatter
back office
backpack
backrest
backroom
back-seat driver
backslide
backspace
backstab
backstage
backstairs
back story
backstroke
backswing
backtalk
backwater
backwoods
backyard

first
first aid
first base
first class
first edition
firsthand
first night
first-rate

second
second base
second best
second class
second-guess
secondhand
secondhand smoke
second-rate
second wind

end
back-end
bitter end
endgame
end line
end matter
endnote
endpaper
end plate
endplay
end product
end run
end table
end use
end user
end zone
front-end

last
last-born
last-ditch
last-gasp
last hurrah
last laugh
last minute
last names
last rites
last straw
last word

Temperature

cold
cold-blooded
cold call
cold cream
cold feet
cold front
cold pack
cold-shoulder
cold sore
cold war

cool
cooldown

coolheaded
cooling tower

hot
hotbed
hot-blooded
hotcake
hothead
hothouse
hot line
hotlink
hot plate
hot seat

hot spot
hot tub
hot-water bottle

warm
warm-blooded
warmed-over
warm front
warm-hearted
warming pan
warm-up

Weather

ice
ice age
iceberg
iceboat
icebound
icebreaker
icecap
icefall
ice field
ice floe
ice fog
ice-free
icehouse
ice pack
ice storm

rain
rainbow
rain check
raincoat
rain date
rainfall

rain forest
rain gauge
rainmaking
rainsquall
rainstorm
rainwater
rainwear

snow
snowball
snowbank
snow blindness
snow blower
snowbound
snowcap
snow cover
snowdrift
snowfall
snowfield
snowflake
snow goose
snow line

snowmaker
snowmelt
snowplow
snowshoe
snowslide
snowstorm
snowsuit
snow tire

wind
wind farm
windmill
windscreen
wind shear
windshield
windsock
windstorm
windsurf
windswept
wind tunnel
wind turbine

Target

Four Elements

air
airbag
airborne
airbrake
airbrush
air chamber
air conditioning
air-cool
air cover
aircraft
airfield
airflow
airfoil
air force
airlift
airline
airlock
airplane
air pocket
airpower
air pressure
air raid
airsick
airspace
airstrip
air taxi
airtight
airwave

earth
earthborn
earthbound
earthenware

earthquake
earth-shaking
earth tone
earthworm

fire
fire alarm
fire ant
firearm
fireball
firebird
fireboard
fireboat
firebomb
firebox
firebrand
firecracker
fire department
fire door
fire drill
fire engine
fire escape
fire extinguisher
firefighter
firefly
fireguard
firehouse
fire hydrant
firelight
fireplace
fireplug
fireproof
fire sale

fire station
fire storm
fire tower
firetrap
firewall
fireworks

water
water ballet
waterbed
water bird
water biscuit
waterborne
water buffalo
water bug
watercolor
watercourse
water cycle
waterfowl
waterfront
water gate
water level
waterline
waterlogged
watermark
water polo
water-repellent
watershed
water supply
watertight
waterwheel
waterworks

Connection

free

free agent
free-associate
free association
freeborn
freedom fighter
freedom rider
free enterprise
free-fall
free flight
free-floating
free-for-all
freeform

freehand
freeload
free market
free-range
free skating
free speech
free-spoken
freestanding
freestyle
freethinker
free trade
free verse
freeway

free will
free world

tied

tieback
tie beam
tiebreaker
tie clasp
tie-in
tie line
tie rod
tie tack
tie-up

Life and Death

dead

dead air
deadbeat
deadbolt
dead end
dead heat
dead language
deadline
deadlock
dead reckoning
dead spot
dead weight

death

deathbed

death benefit
death mask
death rate
death squad
deathtrap
death warrant

life

lifeblood
lifeboat
life cycle
life expectancy
life form
lifeguard
life insurance

life jacket
lifeline
life mask
life preserver
life-size
lifespan
lifestyle
life support
lifetime

live

livelong
livestock

Media

computer
computer age
computer crime
computer graphics
computer language
computer literacy
computer science
computer virus

news
news agency
newsbreak

newscast
news conference
news flash
news group
newsletter
newsmagazine
newsmaker
newspaper
newsprint
news radio
news release

newsroom
newsstand
newsweekly
newswire
newsworthy

radio
radiophone
radiophoto
radiotelegraph
radiotelephone
radio wave

Places

city
city council
city desk
city editor
city hall
city room
cityscape
cityslicker
city-state
citywide

civil
civil defense
civil disobedience
civil engineer

civil law
civil rights
civil servant
civil service
civil war

county
county agent
county fair
county seat
countywide

state
statecraft
statehouse

stateroom
state's evidence
stateside
statesperson
states' rights
statewide

country
back country
country club
country cousin
country music
countryside
countrywide

CLIPPED WORDS

A clipped word is a short word formed from a longer word by dropping one or more syllables.

Easy

Clipped	Standard	Clipped	Standard
bike	bicycle	photo	photograph
hippo	hippopotamus	plane	airplane
phone	telephone	rhino	rhinoceros

Target

Clipped	Standard	Clipped	Standard
ad	advertisement	lab	laboratory
auto	automobile	limo	limousine
bra	brassiere	lunch	luncheon
burger	hamburger	math	mathematics
bus	omnibus	memo	memorandum
champ	champion	movie	moving picture
con	convict	pants	pantaloons
dorm	dormitory	pen	penitentiary
e-mail	electronic mail	pike	turnpike
exam	examination	pop	popular
ex	ex-husband or ex-wife	prom	promenade
		ref	referee
ex-con	ex-convict	sitcom	situation comedy
exec	executive	sub	submarine
an	fanatic	taxi	taxicab
flu	influenza	teen	teenager
fridge	refrigerator	tie	necktie
gas	gasoline	tux	tuxedo
grad	graduate	van	caravan
gym	gymnasium	vet	veterinarian; veteran

Challenge

Clipped	Standard	Clipped	Standard
amp	amplifier	mum	chrysanthemum
cab	cabriolet	perk	perquisite
cam	camera	prenup	prenuptial agreement
cap	capital letter	psych	psychology
carb	carbohydrate	quad	quadrangle
cat	catamaran	recap	recapitulate
chemist	alchemist	rehab	rehabilitation
coed	coeducational	scrip	prescription
condo	condominium	specs	specifications
co-op	cooperative apartment building or business	stats	statistics
		stereo	stereophonic
		synch	synchronize
decaf	decaffeinated	typo	typographical error
demo	demonstration	varsity	university
dub	double	vent	ventilator
fax	facsimile	webcam	Web camera
meds	medications	zoo	zoological gardens

COMMON ABBREVIATIONS

An abbreviation is a shortened form of a word used primarily in writing to represent the whole word.

Easy

Days of the Week

Abbreviation	Whole Word
Mon.	Monday
Tues.	Tuesday
Weds.	Wednesday
Thurs.	Thursday
Fri.	Friday
Sat.	Saturday
Sun.	Sunday

Months*

Abbreviation	Whole Word
Jan.	January
Feb.	February
Mar.	March
Apr.	April
Jun.	June
Jul.	July
Aug.	August
Sept.	September
Oct.	October
Nov.	November
Dec.	December

* There is no abbreviation for May.

Streets and Roads

Abbreviation	Whole Word
Ave.	Avenue
Blvd.	Boulevard
Dr.	Drive
Pl.	Place
Rd.	Road
St.	Street

Titles of Address

Abbreviation	Whole Word
Capt.	Captain
Col.	Colonel
Dr.	Doctor
Gen.	General
Hon.	Honorable
Jr.	Junior
Lt.	Lieutenant
Mr.	Mister
Mrs.	Mistress (for a married woman)
Ms.	Ms. (pronounced "miz," for women who prefer not to be called Mrs. or Miss)
Prof.	Professor
Rev.	Reverend
Sr.	Senior
Sgt.	Sergeant

Target

Time

Abbreviation	Whole Word
A.M.	ante meridiem, "before midday"
P.M.	post meridiem, "after midday"
A.D.	anno Domini, "in the year of our Lord"
B.C.	before Christ
B.C.C.	before the common era
C.E.	common era

Time Zones in U.S.

Abbreviation	Whole Word
EDT	Eastern Daylight Time
EST	Eastern Standard Time
CDT	Central Daylight Time
CST	Central Standard Time
MDT	Mountain Daylight Time
MST	Mountain Standard Time
PDT	Pacific Daylight Time
PST	Pacific Standard Time
AKDT	Alaskan Daylight Time
AKST	Alaskan Standard Time
HADT	Hawaiian-Aleutian Daylight Time
HAST	Hawaiian-Aleutian Standard Time
DST	Daylight Saving Time

U.S./United States

Abbreviation	Whole Word
AL	Alabama
AK	Alaska
AZ	Arizona
AR	Arkansas
CA	California
CO	Colorado
CT	Connecticut
DE	Delaware
FL	Florida
GA	Georgia
HI	Hawaii
ID	Idaho
IL	Illinois
IN	Indiana
IA	Iowa
KS	Kansas
KY	Kentucky
LA	Louisiana
ME	Maine
MD	Maryland
MA	Massachusetts
MI	Michigan
MN	Minnesota
MS	Mississippi
MO	Missouri
MT	Montana
NE	Nebraska
NV	Nevada
NH	New Hampshire
NJ	New Jersey
NM	New Mexico
NY	New York

U.S./United States

Abbreviation	Whole Word
NC	North Carolina
ND	North Dakota
OH	Ohio
OK	Oklahoma
OR	Oregon
PA	Pennsylvania
RI	Rhode Island
SC	South Carolina
SD	South Dakota
TN	Tennessee
TX	Texas
UT	Utah
VT	Vermont
VA	Virginia
WA	Washington
WV	West Virginia
WI	Wisconsin
WY	Wyoming
DC	District of Columbia federal district (Washington D.C.)
AS	American Samoa
FM	Federated States of Micronesia
GU	Guam
MH	Marshall Islands
MP	Northern Mariana Islands
PW	Palau
PR	Puerto Rico
VI	U.S. Virgin Islands

Measurements U.S. System

Length

Abbreviation	Whole Word
in.	inch
ft.	foot
yd.	yard
rd.	rod
fur.	furlong
mi.	mile

Area

Abbreviation	Whole Word
sq. ft.	square foot
sq. yd.	square yard
sq. rd.	square rod
sq. mi.	square mile

Volume

Abbreviation	Whole Word
cu. ft.	cubic foot
cu. yd.	cubic yard

Capacity

Abbreviation	Whole Word
tsp.	teaspoon
tbsp.	tablespoon
oz.	ounce
c.	cup
pt.	pint
qt.	quart
gal.	gallon

Weight

Abbreviation	Whole Word
dr.	dram
oz.	ounce
lb.	pound
cwt	hundredweight
T	ton

Measurements Metric System

Length

Abbreviation	Whole Word
m	meter
dm	decimeter
cm	centimeter
mm	millimeter
dam	dekameter
hm	hectometer
km	kilometer

Area

Abbreviation	Whole Word
sq cm or cm^2	square centimeter
sq km or km^2	square kilometer
ha	hectare

Volume

Abbreviation	Whole Word
m^3	cubic meter
dm^3	cubic decimeter
cc or cu cm or cm^3	cubic centimeter

Capacity

Abbreviation	Whole Word
l	liter
dl	deciliter
cl	centiliter
ml	milliliter
dal	dekaliter
hl	hectoliter
kl	kiloliter
dm^3	cubic decimeter

Weight

Abbreviation	Whole Word
g	gram
dg	decigram
cg	centigram
mg	milligram
kg	kilogram
hg	hectogram
dag	dekagram
t	metric ton

Challenge

Countries of the World

The following two-letter and three-letter codes were established by the International Organization for Standardization (ISO). Country codes are often used at the end of international URLs.

Africa

2-Letter Code	3-Letter Code	Whole Word	2-Letter Code	3-Letter Code	Whole Word
DZ	DZA	Algeria	LS	LSO	Lesotho
AD	AND	Angola	LR	LBR	Liberia
BJ	BEN	Benin	LY	LBY	Libya
BW	BWA	Botswana	MG	MDG	Madagascar
BF	BFA	Burkina Faso	MW	MWI	Malawi
BI	BDI	Burundi	ML	MLI	Mali
CM	CMR	Cameroon	MR	MRT	Mauritania
CV	CPV	Cape Verde	MU	MUS	Mauritius
CF	CAF	Central African Republic	MA	MAR	Morocco
TD	TCD	Chad	MZ	MOZ	Mozambique
KM	COM	Comoros	NA	NAM	Namibia
CD	COD	The Democratic Republic of the Congo	NE	NER	Niger
			NG	NGA	Nigeria
CG	COG	The Republic of the Congo	RW	RWA	Rwanda
CI	CIV	Ivory Coast	ST	STR	Sao Tome and Principe
DJ	DJI	Djibouti	SN	SEN	Senegal
EG	EGY	Egypt	SC	SYC	Seychelles
GQ	GNQ	Equatorial Guinea	SL	SLE	Sierra Leone
ER	ERT	Eritrea	SO	SOM	Somalia
ET	ETH	Ethiopia	ZA	ZAF	South Africa
GA	GAB	Gabon	SD	SDN	Sudan
GM	GMB	Gambia	SZ	SQZ	Swaziland
GH	GHA	Ghana	TZ	TZA	Tanzania
GN	GIN	Guinea	TG	TGO	Togo
GW	GNB	Guinea-Bissau	TN	TUN	Tunisia
KE	KEN	Kenya	UG	UGA	Uganda
			ZM	ZMB	Zambia
			ZW	ZWE	Zimbabwe

Asia

2-Letter Code	3-Letter Code	Whole Word	2-Letter Code	3-Letter Code	Whole Word
AF	AFG	Afghanistan	LB	LBN	Lebanon
AR	ARM	Armenia	MY	MYS	Malaysia
AZ	AZE	Azerbaijan	MV	MDV	Maldives
BH	BHR	Bahrain	MN	MNG	Mongolia
BD	BGD	Bangladesh	MM	MMR	Myanmar
BT	BTN	Bhutan	NP	NPL	Nepal
KH	KHM	Cambodia	OM	OMN	Oman
CN	CHN	China	PK	PAK	Pakistan
CY	CYB	Cyprus	PH	PHL	Philippines
TP	TMP	East Timor	QA	QAT	Qatar
GE	GEO	Georgia	RU	RUS	Russia (also Europe)
IN	IND	India			
ID	IDN	Indonesia	SA	SAU	Saudi Arabia
IR	IRN	Iran	SG	SGP	Singapore
IQ	IRQ	Iraq	LK	LKA	Sri Lanka
IL	ISR	Israel	SY	SYR	Syria
JR	JRN	Japan	TW	TWN	Taiwan
JO	JOR	Jordan	TJ	TJK	Tajikistan
KZ	KAZ	Kazakhstan	TH	THA	Thailand
KP	PRK	Democratic Peoples Republic of Korea (North Korea)	TR	TUR	Turkey (also Europe)
			TM	TKM	Turkmenistan
KR	KOR	Republic of Korea (South Korea)	AE	ARE	United Arab Emirates
KW	KWT	Kuwait	UZ	UZB	Uzbekistan
KG	KGZ	Kyrgyzstan	VN	VNM	Vietnam
LA	LAO	Laos	YE	YEM	Yemen

Australia and Pacific Islands

2-Letter Code	3-Letter Code	Whole Word	2-Letter Code	3-Letter Code	Whole Word
AU	AUS	Australia	PW	PLW	Palau
BN	BRN	Brunei	PG	PNG	Papua New Guinea
FJ	FJL	Fiji			
KI	KIR	Kiribati	WS	WSM	Samoa
MH	MHI	Marshall Islands	SB	SLB	Solomon Islands
FM	FSM	Micronesia	TO	TON	Tonga
NR	NRU	Nauru	TV	TUV	Tuvalu
NZ	NZL	New Zealand	VU	VUT	Vanuatu

Europe

2-Letter Code	3-Letter Code	Whole Word	2-Letter Code	3-Letter Code	Whole Word
AL	ALB	Albania	LU	LUX	Luxembourg
AD	AND	Andorra	MK	MKD	Macedonia
AT	AUT	Austria	MT	MLT	Malta
BY	BLR	Belarus	MD	MDA	Moldova
BE	BEL	Belgium	MC	MCO	Monaco
BO	BIH	Bosnia and Herzegovina	NL	NLD	Netherlands
			NO	NOR	Norway
BG	BGR	Bulgaria	PL	POL	Poland
HR	HRV	Croatia	PT	PRT	Portugal
CZ	CZE	Czech Republic	RO	ROM	Romania
DK	DNK	Denmark	RU	RUS	Russia (also Asia)
EE	EST	Estonia			
FI	FIN	Finland	SM	SMR	San Marino
FR	FRA	France	SK	SVK	Slovakia
DE	DEV	Germany	SI	SVN	Slovenia
GR	GRC	Greece	ES	ESP	Spain
HU	HUN	Hungary	SE	SWE	Sweden
IS	ISL	Iceland	CH	CHE	Switzerland
IE	IRL	Ireland	TR	TUR	Turkey (also Asia)
IT	ITA	Italy	UA	UKR	Ukraine
LV	LVA	Latvia	GB	GBR	United Kingdom (Great Britain)
LI	LIE	Liechtenstein			
LT	LTU	Lithuania	VA	VAT	Vatican City

North America, Central America, and the Caribbean

2-Letter Code	3-Letter Code	Whole Word	2-Letter Code	3-Letter Code	Whole Word
AI	AIA	Anguilla	HN	HND	Honduras
AG	ATG	Antigua and Babuda	JM	JAM	Jamaica
			MX	MEX	Mexico
AW	ABW	Aruba	NI	NIC	Nicaragua
BS	BHS	the Bahamas	PA	PAN	Panama
BB	BRB	Barbados	KN	KNA	Saint Kitts and Nevis
BZ	BLZ	Belize			
BM	BMU	Bermuda	LC	LCA	Saint Lucia
CA	CAN	Canada	VC	VCT	Saint Vincent and the Grenadines
CR	CRI	Costa Rica			
CU	CUB	Cuba	TT	TTO	Trinidad and Tobago
DM	DMA	Dominica			
DO	DOM	Dominican Republic	TC	TCA	Turks and Caicos Islands
SV	SLV	El Salvador	US	USA	United States
GL	GRL	Greenland	BG	VGB	Virgin Islands (British)
GD	GRD	Grenada			
GT	GTM	Guatemala	VI	VIR	Virgin Islands (U.S.)
HT	HTI	Haiti			

South America and Antarctica

2-Letter Code	3-Letter Code	Whole Word	2-Letter Code	3-Letter Code	Whole Word
AR	ARG	Argentina	GY	GUY	Guyana
BO	BOL	Bolivia	PY	PRY	Paraguay
BR	BRA	Brazil	PE	PER	Peru
CL	CHL	Chile	SR	SUR	Suriname
CO	COL	Columbia	UY	URY	Uruguay
EC	ECU	Ecuador	VE	VEN	Venezuela
FK	FLK	Falkland Islands			
GF	GUF	French Guiana	AQ	ATA	Antarctica

ACRONYMS AND INITIALISMS

Acronyms and initialisms are special types of abbreviated words. An acronym is a new word formed from the initial letters of the original words. The word that is formed is pronounced (for example, *radar*). An initialism is formed from the letters of one or more words. For initialisms, the letters are pronounced (for example, *CD*).

Easy

Acronyms (pronounce word)

New Word	Initial letters/Original words
radar	RAdio Detecting And Ranging
scuba	Self-Contained Underwater Breathing Apparatus
sonar	SOund NAvigation and Ranging
UNESCO	United Nations Educational, Scientific, and Cultural Organization
UNICEF	United Nations (International) Children's (Emergency) Fund
ZIP (code)	Zone Improvement Plan

Initialisms (pronounce letters)

Letters	Word(s)
CD	Compact Disc
C.O.D.	Cash On Delivery
FAQ	Frequently Asked Questions
IOU	I Owe You
P.S.	Post Script
TV	TeleVision
TGIF	Thank God (or Goodness) It's Friday

Target

Acronyms (pronounce word)

New Word	Initial letters/Original words	New Word	Initial letters/Original words
AIDS	Acquired Immune Deficiency Syndrome	PIN	Personal Identification Number
AWOL	Absence WithOut Leave	NATO	North Atlantic Treaty Organization
FEMA	Federal Emergency MAnagement Organization	snafu	Situation Normal All Fouled Up
laser	Light Amplification by the Stimulated Emission of Radiation	Teflon	Tetrafloroetylene resin

Initialisms (pronounce letters)

Letters	Words	Letters	Words
AAA	American Automobile Association	IRS	Internal Revenue Service
ABC	American Broadcasting Company	MIA	Missing In Action
ASAP	As Soon As Possible	MO	Modus Operandi (method of operating)
ATM	Automatic Teller Machine	NAACP	National Association for the Advancement of Colored People
BLT	Bacon Lettuce and Tomato sandwich	NBC	National Broadcasting Company
CBS	Columbia Broadcasting System	PBS	Public Broadcasting System
CIA	Central Intelligence Agency	RIP	Rest In Peace
DA	District Attorney	RSVP	Repondez S'il Vous Plait (please respond)
CPR	CardioPulmonary Resuscitation	POW	Prisoner Of War
DJ	Disc Jockey	SAT	Scholastic Achievement (or Aptitude) Test
DNA	DeoxyriboNucleic Acid	SUV	Sports Utility Vehicle
DVD	Digital Video Disc	URL	Uniform Resource Locator
FBI	Federal Bureau of Investigation	VCR	Video Cassette Recorder
FCC	Federal Communications Commission	VIP	Very Important Person
FTC	Federal Trade Commission	VJ	Video Jockey
IQ	Intelligence Quotient		

Combination Acronym and Initialism

CD-ROM	Compact Disc Read Only Memory	Q-and-A	Question-and-Answer

Challenge

Acronyms (pronounce word)

New word	Initial letters/Original words
BASIC	Beginner's All-purpose Symbolic Instruction Code
CAD	Computer-Aided Design
CAT	Computerized Axial Tomography
DOS	Disc Operating System

New word	Initial letters/Original words
Ginny Mae	Government National Mortgage Association
HUD	Department of Housing and Urban Development
NAFTA	North American Free Trade Agreement

Initialisms (pronounce letters)

Letters	Words
AI	Artificial intelligence
AKA	Also Known As
BBC	British Broadcasting System
CEO	Chief Executive Officer
CFO	Chief Financial Officer
DNA	DeoxyriboNucleic Acid
EU	European Union

Letters	Words
GNP	Gross National Product
GPA	Grade Point Average
GPS	Global Positioning System
LCD	Liquid Crystal Display
LED	Light Emitting Diode
NEA	National Endowment for the Arts

Combination Acronym and Initialism

JPEG	Joint Photographic Experts Group

WORDS FROM MYTHOLOGY

Greek , Roman, and Norse myths have provided a rich source of words in English, including the days of the week, character traits, and scientific concepts.

Easy

Days

Word	Origin	Meaning
Sunday	from Sunne, Norse goddess of the sun	the Sun's day; first day of the week
Monday	from Mani, the Norse god of the moon	the Moon's day; second day of the week
Tuesday	from Tyr or Tiu, the Norse god of war	third day of the week
Wednesday	from Woden, king of the Norse gods and god of the hunt	fourth day of the week
Thursday	from Thor, the Norse god of thunder	fifth day of the week
Friday	from Freyja, the Norse goddess of love	sixth day of the week
Saturday	from Saturn, the Roman god of agriculture who reigned during the Golden Age	seventh day of the week

Months

Word	Origin	Meaning
January	from Janus, the Roman god of doorways, who had two faces—one looking backward and one forward	first month of the year
March	from Mars, the Roman god of war	third month of the year
May	from Maia, in Greek mythology, one of the seven daughters of Atlas, and the mother of Mercury	fifth month of the year
June	from Juno, the Roman goddess of marriage, who was queen and wife of Jupiter;	sixth month of the year

Flora and Fauna

Word	Origin	Meaning
floral	from Flora, the Roman goddess of flowers	of, relating to, or showing flowers
hyacinth	from Hyacinthus, a Spartan youth beloved by the Greek gods,	a plant that has a thick stem with small flowers that grow in long clusters
iris	from the Greek, goddess of the rainbow	a plant with long, thin leaves and large purple, white, or yellow flowers
mint	from Minthe, a Greek nymph transformed into an herb by the goddess Persephone	an herb whose leaves have a strong scent and are used for flavoring
narcissus	from Narcissus, the Greek youth who fell in love with his own image in a pool of water, fell in and drowned, and was turned into a flower	a plant that has yellow or white flowers and long, thin leaves (a daffodil is a kind of narcissus)
peony	from Paeon, the physician to the gods in Greek mythology	a garden plant with large flowers that may be red, pink, or white

Geography

Word	Origin	Meaning
Asia	from the Greek goddess Asia, the mother of Atlas	the world's largest continent
atlas	from the Greek Titan condemned to stand at the end of the world and hold up the sky	a book of maps
Europe	from the princess Europa, in Greek mythology, who was abducted by Zeus and carried from Phoenicia to Crete	the world's second-smallest continent, after Australia
ocean	from Oceanus, Greek god of the great waters	the entire body of salt water that covers most of the earth's surface
volcano	from Vulcan, the Roman god of fire and blacksmiths	a mountain with vents through which molten lava, ash, cinders, and gas erupt

Planets

Word	Origin	Meaning
Mercury	from the Roman god Mercury, the fleet-footed messenger of the gods and of business	planet closest to the Sun

Word	Origin	Meaning
Venus	from Venus, the Roman goddess of love and beauty	second planet from the Sun
Mars	from Mars, the Roman god of war	fourth planet from the Sun
Jupiter	from Jupiter, the Roman god who was ruler of the other Roman gods	fifth planet from the Sun
Saturn	from the Roman god Saturn, the father of Jupiter	sixth planet from the Sun
Uranus	from the Greek god Uranus, who was the earliest and supreme god	seventh planet from the Sun
Neptune	from the Roman god of the sea, Neptune	eighth planet from the Sun
Pluto	from the Roman god of the underworld, Pluto	a dwarf planet, formerly classified as the ninth planet from the Sun

Target

Appearance, Character Traits, and Behavior

Word	Origin	Meaning
Achilles' heel	from the Greek hero Achilles, whose when he was a baby, dipped him in magical water to protect him, but did not remove her hand from his heel	weak spot
berserk	from legendary Norse warrior, Old Berserkr, known for his ferociousness and frenzy in battle	violent, upset, and destructive
hector	from Hector, the Trojan prince killed by Achilles	bully; threaten
jovial	from Jove, another name for Jupiter, the chief Roman god	cheerful; jolly
Junoesque	from Juno, the Roman queen of the gods and wife of Jupiter	stately and imposing
juvenile	from Juventus, Roman god of youth	young; immature
lunatic	from Luna, Roman goddess of the moon	someone who is crazy

Word	Origin	Meaning
martial	from Mars, the Roman god of war	warlike
mercurial	from the Roman god Mercury, the fleet-footed messenger of the gods and of business	quick and changeable in mood
panic	from the Greek god Pan, the god of sheep and of dark woods and fields	sudden, intense fear
promethean	from the Greek Titan Prometheus, who stole fire from the gods	wildly creative; defiant and bold
tantalize	from the Greek king Tantalus, who was condemned to stand in water that he couldn't drink, with fruit above him that he couldn't reach	to tempt someone without letting that person have what he or she desires

Objects, Occupations, and Other Things

Word	Origin	Meaning
ambrosia	from ambrosia, the food of the gods, thought to give immortality to those who eat it	a sweet treat with oranges and flaked coconut
calliope	from Kalliope, the Greek muse with a beautiful voice, who watched over epic poetry	a keyboard instrument like an organ but fitted with steam whistles
cereal	from Ceres, Roman goddess of grain	a breakfast food
chronology	from Chronos, Roman god of time	order of events
kraken	from the Norse sea monster, the Kraken	a sea monster
mentor	from Mentor, a trusted advisor to Odysseus	an advisor; someone who takes you under his/her wing
merchandise	from the Roman god Mercury, the fleet-footed messenger of the gods and of business	things that are bought and sold
merchant	from the Roman god Mercury, the fleet-footed messenger of the gods and of business	someone in the business of selling things
museum	from the nine Muses in Greek mythology, who presided over the arts and sciences	a place for viewing and studying objects of artistic, historic, and scientific interest

Word	Origin	Meaning
music	from the nine Muses in Greek mythology, who presided over the arts and sciences	the arrangement of sounds to create an artistic piece
pontoon	from Pontus, the Greek god of the sea	a type of floating structure or bridge
siren	from the Sirens, Greek sea nymphs who lured sailors to their doom	an alarm or distress signal
terminal	from Terminus, the Roman guardian of boundaries	an end point or station
typhoon	from Typhon, a rebellious Greek god who ruled destructive volcanoes and storms	a hurricane or violent tropical storm in the western Pacific or Indian Ocean
zephyr	from Zephyrus, the Greek god of the west wind	a gentle breeze

Qualities, Magnitude, and Ideas

Word	Origin	Meaning
colossal	from the Colossus of Rhodes, a huge statue of the Greek god Apollo	extremely large and awe inspiring
cupidity	from Cupid, the god of love and son of the Roman goddess Venus	greed; intense desire
discord	from Discordia, the Roman goddess of disagreement	disagreement; strife
fortune	from Fortuna, the Roman goddess of luck	luck; fate; destiny
fury	from the Furies, three Greek goddesses who sought out and punished wrongdoers	anger and rage
herculean	from Hercules, the Greek hero of exceptional strength who accomplished twelve seemingly impossible tasks	demanding great strength and effort
iridescent	from Iris, the Greek goddess of the rainbow	brilliant; sparkling; showing the colors of the rainbow
Midas touch	from Midas, who, in Greek myths, turned everything he touched into gold	the ability to make huge amounts of money

Word	Origin	Meaning
narcissism	from Narcissus, the Greek youth who fell in love with his own image in a pool of water	intense self-love and admiration
odyssey	from Odysseus, the Greek hero who, after the Trojan War, traveled for many years to get back to his home	a long voyage filled with adventures
Olympian	from Mt. Olympus, the home of the Greek gods	exalted; majestic
panacea	from Panacea, a daughter of Aesculpius, the Greek god of medicine	a cure-all or universal remedy
saturnine	from the Roman god Saturn, the father of Jupiter	dark and threatening
Stygian	from the River Styx in the underworld of Greek mythology	dark, gloomy, and forebidding
titanic	from the Titans, the family of giants who, in Greek mythology, originally ruled the heavens	colossal; extraordinarily large and strong

Challenge

Character Types

Word	Origin	Meaning
Adonis	from the beautiful youth loved by the Greek goddess Aphrodite	a strikingly beautiful man
amazon	from the women warriors of Greek mythology	a particularly strong, tall, and aggressive woman
Cassandra	from the daughter of King Priam and Queen Hecuba of Troy	a person who predicts misfortunes but is not believed
nemesis	from Nemesis, the Greek goddess of justice or vengeance	someone who keeps pursuing another to get justice; a force that cannot be beaten

Science and Health

Word	Origin	Meaning
arachnid	from Arachne, a Greek girl changed into a spider by Athena	a spider
chimera	from a fire-breathing monster in Greek mythology made up of a goat, a lion, and a serpent	a highly fanciful illusion; or an organism made up of different genetic tissues
echoic	from Echo, the Greek nymph who pined away for her lover until only her voice remained	relating to the repetition of sound by reflection of sound waves off a surface
electricity	from Electra, the daughter of Agamemnon, who, in Greek mythology, avenged her father's death	a phenomenon arising from the behavior of electrons and protons
fauna	from Fauna, the Roman goddess of birth and fertility	the animal life in a particular region
flora	from Flora, the Roman goddess of spring and flowers	the plant life in a particular region
helium	from Helios, the Greek titan who was the sun god	the lightest element
hygiene	from Hygeia, the Greek goddess of health and cleanliness	the science dealing with health and cleanliness
hypnosis	from Hypnos, the Greek god of sleep	the technique of putting someone in an induced, trancelike condition

WORDS BASED ON NAMES OF PEOPLE

Many words have been coined from the names of people. Often, these people invented, discovered, or did something special that brought about the word. Words coined from people's names are called eponyms.

Easy

Word	Person	Meaning
America	from Amerigo Vespucci, one of the European explorers of the New World	the great landmasses that make up what is now North America, Central America, and South America
braille	from Louis Braille, a French teacher of the blind who was himself blind	a system of writing consisting of raised dot-formed letters that can be read by touch
cardigan	from James Thomas Brudenell, seventh Earl of Cardigan, an English soldier who led the Charge of the Light Brigade and whose soldiers wore this type of garment	a longed-sleeved buttoned sweater without a collar
Morse code	from the American inventor of the telegraph, Samuel Finley Breese Morse	a dot-dash code system used by telegraphers to send messages
sandwich	from John Montagu, the fourth Earl of Sandwich, who reputedly put slices of meat between bread so that he could keep gambling without being interrupted by eating	two or more slices of bread with a filling in-between
teddy bear	from Theodore Roosevelt, 26th president of United States and noted outdoorsman, who reputedly refused to shoot a bear cub	a stuffed toy bear
valentine	from St. Valentine, an early Christian martyr whose feast day falls on Feb. 14, the day, according to some old legends, when birds begin to mate	a holiday during which sweethearts express affection

Target

Word	Person	Meaning
argyle	from the Duke of Argyle	a brightly colored diamond-shaped cloth pattern resembling the Argyle Clan tartan

Word	Person	Meaning
bloomers	from Amelia Jenks Bloomer, an American feminist and social reformer who wore these pantaloons	full, loose trousers that are gathered at the ankle or knee
bobby	from Sir Robert Peel, the British Home Secretary who reorganized the London police force	a police officer; a member of the London police force
bowie knife	from Col. James Bowie, a Texas patriot and soldier, who popularized the knife and marketed it under his name	a knife with a double-edged blade that curved to a point
boycott	from Charles Cunningham Boycott, an Irish landlord whose tenants refused to pay rents and who was refused services in local stores in protest against harsh conditions	to avoid trade or refuse to deal with, as a protest
Bunsen burner	from Robert Wilhelm Bunsen, who invented it	used in most chemistry labs, a burner that mixes gas with air to produce a hot flame
colt	from Samuel Colt, who invented this gun	a six-shooter or revolver
derby	from Edward Stanley, 12th Earl of Derby, who had a strong interest in horse racing	a dome-shaped felt hat also called a bowler that was created to look like the bowler hats the English wore at the Derby (a horse race, also named for him)
derrick	from Godfrey Derrick, a 16th-century English executioner known for his strength	a crane for lifting heavy objects
derringer	from Henry Derringer, the Philadelphia gunsmith who invented it	a small, stubby, easily hidden pistol
diesel	from Rudolf Diesel, a German engineer who built the engine that bears his name	a type of internal combustion engine
Ferris wheel	from George Washington Gail Ferris whose invention debuted at the Columbian Exposition in Chicago in 1893	a giant wheel with passenger-carrying cars that revolves on a stationary axis or stand
gibberish	from Geber, or Jabir ibn Hayyan, an Arabian alchemist who, as a precaution against being charged with sorcery, wrote in seemingly unintelligible code	nonsense language
guillotine	from Dr. Joseph-Ignace Guillotin, a French physician who proposed its use during the French Revolution	a machine with a sharp sliding blade used for beheading people
hooligan	from Patrick Hooligan, a rowdy 19th-century criminal and thug	a ruffian or other violent thug

Word	Person	Meaning
leotard	from Jules Leotard, a 19th-century French aerial gymnast	a close-fitting one-piece garment worn by dancers and gymnasts
Levi's	from Levi Strauss, a San Francisco manufacturer who made these sturdy pants during the Gold Rush	jeans; dungarees
lynch	from Charles Lynch, a Virginia planter who formed a secret band to punish people accused of crimes	to hang someone for a crime without benefit of a trial
macintosh	from Charles Macintosh, a Scottish chemist who patented a method for making waterproof garments	a kind of raincoat
magnolia	from Pierre Magnol, a French physician and botanist who classified plants	an evergreen tree with showy flowers
mason jar	from John L. Mason, an American manufacturer who invented and patented them	a heavy glass jar used for home canning and preserving
maverick	from Samuel Augustus Maverick, a Texas lawyer and rancher who claimed ownership of any unbranded cattle	unbranded cattle; a nonconformist
pasteurize	from Louis Pasteur, a French scientist who invented the process of pasteurization	a process to purify and preserve milk by heating and rapid cooling
ritzy	from César Ritz, Swiss restaurateur and hotel manager who built a lavish hotel	classy, lavish, expensive
shrapnel	from Henry Shrapnel, an English military officer who invented a specific type of exploding projectile	fragments of an exploding artillery shell or bomb
sideburns	from General Ambrose Burnside, who wore the hair on the side of his face in a distinctive way (originally called burnsides)	long hair growing on the side of a man's face
silhouette	from Etienne de Silhouette, a French finance minister, who placed severe restrictions on spending and whose name became associated with being cheap	an outline image filled in with black
spaldeen	from Alfred Goodwell Spalding, who established manufacturing standards for baseballs and baseball equipment	a rubber ball
Stetson	from John Batterson Stetson, a hatmaker who specialized in cowboy hats	a hat with a tall crown and wide brim, often called a 10-gallon hat

Challenge

Word	Person	Meaning
bowdlerize	from Thomas Bowdler, editor of an expurgated edition of Shakespeare	to censor or delete written material considered improper or bawdy
camellia	from George Joseph Kamel, a botanist who described the plant he found in the Philippines	a beautiful flowering plant
chauvinism	from Nicolas Chauvin of Rochefort, a French soldier who was extremely patriotic and nationalistic	excessively patriotic or loyal to a group
curie	from Marie and Pierre Curie, French chemists and codiscoverers of radium	a unit of measure for radioactivity
doily	from a London linen merchant named Doily, Doiley, Doylet, or Doyly	a mat made of lace
draconian	from Draco, Athenian ruler and lawgiver who established extremely harsh penalties for crime	harsh application of law or rules
dunce	from John Duns Scotus, a 13th and 14th centuries philosopher whose work was later mocked	a fool or blockhead
forsythia	from William Forsyth, a Scottish gardener who brought the plant to England from China	a shrub with bright yellow flowers
gerrymander	from Elbridge Gerry, Governor of Massachusetts, who approved a politically inspired plan to reshape voting districts	to manipulate or change electoral districts to benefit the party in power
kaiser	from Julius Caesar, Roman general and dictator	emperor; ruler (also czar; tsar)
kelvin scale	from William Thompson, Lord Kelvin, a Scottish scientist who invented this scale	a scale for measuring temperature
klieg lights	from John H. and Anton T. Kliegl, who invented the high-intensity lights used in the early days of filmmaking	high-intensity lights
macadam	from John Loudon McAdam, a road engineer who built these small crushed-stone or gravel roads	a smooth road surface made from stones mixed with asphalt or tar

Word	Person	Meaning
macadamia	from Dr. John Macadam, Secretary of the Victoria Philosophical Institute	a type of tree with nuts
mach number	from Ernst Mach, a German scientist who investigated supersonic speed	the ratio of the speed of an object and the speed of sound in air
machiavellian	from Niccolò Machiavelli, who, in his book *The Prince*, asserted that a ruler may use any means available to maintain power	scheming; using unscrupulous methods to maintain power
madeleine	from Madeleine Paulmier, a French pastry chef who created these cakes	a small shell-shaped cake
mansard	from Nicolas François Mansart, aka Mansard, a French architect and designer	a type of roof that accommodates high-ceiling attics
martinet	from Colonel Jean Martinet, a French officer and strict disciplinarian	a strict, overbearing disciplinarian
marzipan	from Franz Marzip, a German confectioner	a sweet treat made of almond paste and sugar
mausoleum	from King Maussollus of ancient Persia, whose wife ordered a huge monument erected to him after his death	a large tomb
mercerize	from John Mercer, an American industrialist who invented this method for treating cotton cloth	to treat cotton fabric in a way that strengthens it and gives it a silky luster
mesmerize	from Franz Anton Mesmer, an early Austrian hypnotist	to put in a trace-like state; to hypnotize or hold spellbound
minié ball	from Captain Claude Étienne Minié, a French soldier who invented a new kind of lead bullet	a cone-shaped lead bullet
Molotov cocktail	from Vyacheslav Molotov, a Russian statesman who claimed that the bombs the Russians were dropping on the Finns were only food and drink	a crude bomb; a gasoline-filled bottle with a rag fuse
Neanderthal	from Joachim Neander, a poet who wrote in praise of the glory of creation and for whom the Neanderthal (valley) was named	an early form of Homo sapiens
nicotine	from Jean Nicot, the French ambassador to Portugal when tobacco was first brought to Europe from the New World	a byproduct of the combustion of tobacco
obsidian	from Obsius, an ancient Greek explorer who first described it	a kind of volcanic glass

Word	Person	Meaning
ohm	from Georg Ohm, a German scientist who studied electric currents	a unit of electrical resistance
pompadour	from Madame de Pompadour, a French noblewoman who was a Parisian fashion leader and who wore her hair this way	a hairstyle in which hair is swept up from the forehead
petri dish	from Julius Richard Petri, a German scientist who invented this laboratory dish	a flat glass or plastic dish with a loose cover
quisling	from Vidkun Quisling, a fascist who became ruler of Norway after the Nazis invaded the country during World War II	a traitor who is a puppet of the enemy
raglan sleeve	from Fitzroy James Henry Somerset, Ist Baron Raglan, a courageous 18th-century British soldier who wore a loose-fitting coat with sleeves extending to the neck	a style of sleeve that is cut so that it extends to the neck
saxophone	from Antoine Joseph Sax, a Belgian musical instrument maker	a valved brass instrument
spinet	from Giovanni Spinetti, a Venetian musical instrument maker	a small, upright piano
spoonerism	from the Reverend William Archibald Spooner, who was famous for his slips of the tongue	a one-line phrase in which the initial letters of words are switched
tawdry	from St. Audrey (also known as St. Etheldreda) who was honored by holding fairs on her saint's day during which lace scarves and necklaces were sold as souvenirs	cheaply made; gaudy
thespian	from Thespis, a sixth-century Greek poet	an actor
Vandyke	from Sir Anthony Van Dyck, a Flemish painter who depicted noblemen sporting this distinctive style of beard	v-shaped beard
volt	from Count Alessandro Giuseppe Antonio Anastasio Volta, an Italian scientist who invented the first electric battery	a unit of measure of electric force
zeppelin	from Count Ferdinand von Zeppelin, a German designer and Civil War veteran of the Union Army who developed this airship	a rigid, lighter-than-air aircraft

WORDS BASED ON PLACES

Many words have been coined based on the names of places. Often these words refer back to where the item was invented, made, or first found. Words based on places are called toponyms.

Easy

Word	Place	Meaning
Bermuda shorts	from Bermuda	knee-length pants
bologna	from Bologna, Italy	a type of lunch meat
cheddar cheese	from Cheddar, England	a type of hard cheese
china	from China	porcelain dishes
frankfurter	from Frankfurt, Germany	a hot dog
hamburger	from Hamburg, Germany or New York	a meat patty
lumber	from Lombardy, Italy	wood from trees that have been cut down
magnet	from Magnesia, Asia Minor	a piece of metal that has the power to draw iron or steel
palace	from the Palatine Hill, Rome, Italy	a grand residence for monarchs
pistol	from Pistoia, Italy	a gun

Target

Word	Place	Meaning
academy	from the Academia, Athens, Greece	a school
angora	from Ankara, Turkey	wool from a goat or rabbit
arsenal	from the Arsenale, Venice, Italy	a place where weapons are stored
baked Alaska	from Alaska, U.S.A.	a dessert of cake and ice cream with a meringue topping
bikini	from the Bikini Atoll in the South Pacific	a scanty two-piece bathing suit

Word	Place	Meaning
blarney	from a stone in the Blarney Castle, Cork, Ireland	flattery and smooth, but insincere, talk
Brazil nut	from Brazil, South America	a type of tree with edible nuts
Brussels sprouts	from Brussels, Belgium	a type of vegetable
Cajun	from Acadia, Canada	a Louisiana native who is a descendent of French Canadians
calico	from Calicut, India	a type of coarse cloth
cantaloupe	from Cantalupo, Italy	a type of melon
cashmere	from Kashmir, India	wool from a goat
champagne	from the province of Champagne, France	a sparkling wine
Charleston	from Charleston, South Carolina	a type of dance
dalmatian	from Dalmatia, Croatia	a type of dog
denim	from Nîmes, France (de Nîmes)	a coarse cloth used for jeans
duffel bag	from Duffel, Belgium	a large canvas bag
fez	from Fes, Morocco	a flat-topped hat with a tassel
forum	from the Forum in Rome, Italy	a meeting place or public square
gauze	from Gaza in the Middle East	a thin, filmy cloth
ghetto	from the island of Ghetto, Venice, Italy	a racially segregated area or area where specific groups are forced to live
italics	from Italy	a slanted typeface
jersey	from the Isle of Jersey, England	a knitted sweater
java	from Java, Indonesia	coffee
lima bean	from Lima, Peru	a type of edible flat pod; butter bean
limburger cheese	from the Limburg province, Holland	a type of pungent cheese
limerick	from Limerick, Ireland	a humorous five-lined poem
limousine	from Limousin, France	a luxurious vehicle usually driven by a chauffeur
lobby	from the lobby to the British House of Commons, London, England	to influence political representatives to vote a certain way or support a specific cause

Word	Place	Meaning
Louisville slugger	from Louisville, Kentucky	a baseball bat
mackinaw	Macinac City, Michigan	a thick woolen blanket or a coat made from this cloth
manila paper	from Manila, the Philippines	a thick paper or cardboard
mayonnaise	from Port Mahon, Minorca, Spain	a dressing made from egg yolks
milliner	from Milan, Italy	a hat maker
muslin	from Mosul, Iraq	a sturdy cotton fabric
rhinestone	from the Rhine River in Europe	artificial gems
romaine	from Rome, Italy	a type of lettuce
Roman numeral	from Rome, Italy	any of the symbols used by the ancient Romans to represent numbers
spa	from Spa, Belgium	a resort or other place offering health-related activities and treatments
Swiss cheese	from Switzerland	a type of cheese characterized by holes
suede	from Sweden	a type of velvety-surfaced leather
wiener	from Vienna, Austria	a frankfurter

Challenge

Word	Place	Meaning
argosy	from Rugusa, Dalmatia (*rugusa* corrupted to *argosy*)	a large merchant ship or fleet of ships
bohemian	from the Kingdom of Bohemia in Northern Europe	a person with an unconventional lifestyle
coliseum	from the Colosseum in Rome, Italy	a large arena or theater for a sporting event
damascene	from Damascus, Syria	to create a design with wavy patterns on metal
damask	from Damascus, Syria	a cotton or linen patterned fabric
dumdum bullet	from the Dum-Dum Arsenal in Bengal, India	a bullet that expands on impact
homburg	from Homburg, Germany	a soft, felt hat

Word	Place	Meaning
india ink	from India	a type of black ink
japan	from Japan	to decorate with a black enamel
jimsonweed	derived from Jamestown-weed, Jamestown, Virginia	a tall poisonous weed
laconic	from Laconia, Sparta, Greece	terse; not verbose; using few words
Leyden jar	from Leyden, Holland	an early form of a capacitor
Linzer torte	from Linz, Austria	a pastry with a raspberry filling
madras	from Madras, India	a fabric with a striped or checked pattern
maelstrom	from the Maelstrom, a whirlpool off the west coast of Norway	a large whirlpool
magenta	from Magenta, Italy	a reddish-purple color
mecca	from Mecca, Saudi Arabia	a center of activity that draws many people
meringue	from Mirengen, Switzerland	a confection made of egg whites whipped with sugar
organdy	from Urgendi, Turkestan	a cotton or silk lightweight fabric used for dresses
panama hat	from Panama	a brimmed hat made from plaited leaves
parmesan	from Parma, Italy	a type of cheese
rialto	from the Rialto in Venice, Italy	a marketplace or theater district
romanesque	from Rome, Italy	relating to a style of architecture that combines Roman and Byzantine elements
roquefort	from Roquefort, France	a type of blue-veined cheese
sienna	from Siena, Italy	a reddish color
venetian blinds	from Venice, Italy	a window covering with slats that can be adjusted to let light in or keep it out
verdigris	from Greece (literally "green of Greece")	a greenish color found on copper and brass that has oxidized
worsted	from Worsted, England	a type of close-woven woolen cloth

WORDS FROM WARS

Words entered English from different wars. Sometimes a new word was coined. Sometimes the meaning of the word was extended to cover a new object or situation.

Easy

Word	War	Meaning
ace	from World War I	an expert fighter pilot
dogfight	from World War I	an aerial battle between fighter pilots
dog tag	from World War I	a metal identification tag worn by a soldier
GI	from World War II	a soldier who has enlisted
jeep	from World War II	an open four-wheel-drive vehicle
tank	from World War I	an armored vehicle

Target

Word	War	Meaning
A-bomb	from WWII	an atomic bomb
airlift	from the Spanish Civil War	to transport soldiers or other people by air
AWOL	from the Civil War	absent without leave
beachhead	from World War I	territory held on the enemy shoreline and used as a launching point for an attack
blitz (blitzkrieg)	from World War II	an intense, heavy air raid
brainwash	from the Korean War	to impose beliefs through torture or intensive indoctrination
brass hat	from World War I	high-ranking military officer
concentration camp	from World War II	a prison where people are kept under extremely harsh conditions
doughboy	from World War I	a soldier
draftee	from the Civil War	someone conscripted or drafted into military service
gestapo	from World War II	Nazi secret police
gung ho	from World War II	extremely brave, loyal, and eager
joystick	from World War I	an airplane's control stick

Word	War	Meaning
kamikaze	from World War II	Japanese suicide bombers
mushroom cloud	from World War II	the cloud caused by an atomic explosion
nosedive	from World War I	a steep dive or swooping downward of an aircraft
R and R	from World War II	leave granted for rest and recuperation
radar	from World War II	an acronym for *radio detecting and ranging*
shell shock	from World War I	combat fatigue caused by exposure to shell fire
storm trooper	from World War II	a member of the Nazi militia
trench coat	from World War I	a belted, military-style raincoat
U-boat	from World War I	a German submarine
walkie-talkie	from World War II	a portable radio set used for communication
warhorse	from the Civil War	an experienced veteran
watch cap	from World War I	a knitted cap
war correspondent	from the Civil War	someone who reports on a war

Challenge

Word	War	Meaning
balaclava	from the Crimean War	a woolen garment covering the head and neck
bazooka	from World War II	a gun that fires rockets
cravat	from the Thirty Years War	a neckerchief or scarf
fifth columnist	from the Spanish Civil War	a secret agent or saboteur
flattop	from World War II	an aircraft carrier
genocide	from World War II	the planned extermination of an entire race or group of people
medivac	from the Korean War	an acronym for a vehicle used for medical evacuation
pillbox	from World War I	a shelter for a machine gun
pipsqueak	from World War I	a small, fast artillery shell
sabotage	from World War II	to deliberately destroy weapons and equipment
stalag	from World War II	a prisoner-of-war camp
strafe	from World War I	to attack with heavy machine-gun fire from a low-flying airplane

PORTMANTEAU WORDS

In his nonsense poem "Jabberwocky" from *Through the Looking-Glass and What Alice Found There*, Lewis Carroll coined new words by blending sounds from two familiar words. The new word carries the meaning of both the original words and is called a portmanteau word. The process continues to this day.

Easy

Word	Combined Words	Meaning
brunch	breakfast + lunch	a late-morning meal
carjack	car + hijack	to hijack or forcibly take a car from someone
motel	motor + hotel	a casual hotel for motorists
scrunch	squeeze + crunch	to crush tightly together
slosh	slop + slush	to spill or splash in a clumsy manner
smog	smoke + fog	pollution caused by a mixture of fog and smoke
splatter	splash + spatter	to spatter and splash something
squiggle	squirm + wiggle	a wavy line

Target

Word	Combined Words	Meaning
aerobatics	aeroplane + acrobatics	spectacular stunts performed by airplanes
biopic	biography + picture	a movie about a real-life person
chocoholic	chocolate + alcoholic	someone who likes chocolate too much
chortle	chuckle + snort	noisy, hearty laughter
chunnel	Channel + tunnel	the tunnel through the English Channel
emoticon	emotion + icon	a picture used to express emotion
guesstimate	guess + estimate	an estimate based on guessing
heliport	helicopter + airport	an airport for helicopters
moped	motor + pedal	bicycle with a motor
motorcade	motor + cavalcade	a parade or procession of cars and other vehicles
paratrooper	parachute + trooper	a soldier who parachutes into battle
prissy	prim + sissy	excessively prim and proper
prequel	precede + sequel	a sequel that tells what happened before
shopaholic	shop + alcoholic	someone who likes to shop too much
slithy	slimy + lithe	slippery and thin
workaholic	work + alcoholic	someone who works too hard and too much

Challenge

Word	Combined Words	Meaning
advertorial	advertisement + editorial	an editorial written for the purpose of advertising a product or service
animatronics	animation + electronics	cartoons and other animated computer graphics
aquacise	aqua + exercise	exercise routines performed in water
biotech	biology + technology	the use of biology and biological processes for production
camcorder	camera + recorder	a portable video camera and recorder
contrail	condensation + trail	the visible trail of vapor left by an aircraft
cyborg	cybernetic + organism	a creature that is part human and part machine
edutainment	education + entertainment	entertainment created for educational purposes
infomercial	information + commercial	a commercial designed to give a lot of information
netizen	Internet + citizen	citizen of the Internet; Internet user
pixel	picture + element	a computer picture element or image

WORDS SHAKESPEARE ADDED TO THE LANGUAGE

Through his plays and poems, Shakespeare is credited with adding many words to the English language. In some cases, he coined new words. In other cases, he used an existing word as a different part of speech or joined two existing words. In still others, he gave an existing word a new meaning. Shakespeare also gave words from other languages new English forms, and he added prefixes and/or suffixes to existing words to form new words. Some scholars, though, are dubious about the number of words attributed to Shakespeare, claiming that he can be credited only with the earliest written examples of the use of these words that we have. In other words, the words may have been in use before, but no written examples of them exist.

Easy

Word	Usage/Meaning	Shakespeare Connection
alligator	a noun meaning an aquatic reptile	said by Balthasar in *Romeo and Juliet*
bandit	a noun meaning thief, robber	said by the Duke of Suffolk in *Henry VI, Part II*
bedroom	a noun meaning space with a bed for sleeping	said by Lysander in *A Midsummer Night's Dream*
bet	a verb meaning to wager	said by Shallow in *Henry IV, Part II*
blanket	a verb meaning to cover	said by Edgar in *King Lear*
bump	a noun meaning a lump or raised bruise	said by Nurse in *Romeo and Juliet*
dawn	a noun meaning sunrise	said by King Henry in *Henry V*
eyeball	a noun meaning the round mass of the eye	said by Oberon in *A Midsummer Night's Dream*
farmhouse	a noun meaning a dwelling on a farm	said by the Host in *The Merry Wives of Windsor*
hint	a noun meaning a clue	said by Othello in *Othello*
hush	an adjective meaning quiet or still	said by the First Player in *Hamlet*
leapfrog	a noun meaning a game	said by King Henry in *Henry V*
moonbeam	a noun meaning light from the moon	said by Titania in *A Midsummer Night's Dream*

Word	Usage/Meaning	Shakespeare Connection
puppy dog	a noun meaning a young canine	said by Philip in *King John*
roadway	a noun meaning a street or path	said by Prince Hal in *Henry IV, Part II*
unreal	an adjective meaning imaginary	said by Macbeth in *Macbeth*
watchdog	a noun meaning a dog that guards	said by Ariel in *The Tempest*

Target

Word	Usage/Meaning	Shakespeare Connection
accused	a noun meaning a person suspected of a crime	said by the King in *Richard II*
aerial	an adjective meaning in or of the air	said by Montano in *Othello*
amazement	a noun meaning surprise	said by Philip in *King John*
arouse	a verb meaning to awaken	said by the Captain in *Henry VI, Part II*
backing	a noun meaning support	said by Falstaff in *Henry IV, Part I*
barefaced	an adjective meaning obvious	said by Macbeth in *Macbeth*
beached	an adjective meaning having a shore	said by Titania in *A Midsummer Night's Dream*
birthplace	a noun meaning a place where a person is born	said by Coriolanus in *Coriolanus*
bloodstained	an adjective meaning colored by blood	said by Martius in *Titus Andronicus*
blushing	an adjective meaning flushing of the face	said by York in *Henry VI, Part III*
buzzer	a noun meaning a noisemaker	said by Claudius in *Hamlet*
caked	a verb meaning to encrust or harden	said by Timon in *Timon of Athens*
champion	a verb meaning to defy	said by Macbeth in *Macbeth*
cloud-capped	an adjective meaning topped with clouds	said by Prospero in *The Tempest*
coldblooded	an adjective meaning unfeeling	said by Constance in *King John*
compromise	a verb meaning betray	said by Shylock in *The Merchant of Venice*
countless	an adjective meaning too numerous to count	said by Marcus Andronicus in *Titus Andronicus*

Word	Usage/Meaning	Shakespeare Connection
courtship	a noun meaning the activity of courting or wooing	said by the Princess in *Love's Labour's Lost*
critic	a noun meaning one who analyzes or evaluates	said by Berowne in *Love's Labour's Lost*
design	a noun meaning a plan or target	said by Don Adriano de Armado in *Love's Labour's Lost*
dialogue	a verb meaning to talk together or hold a conversation	said by the Maid in *A Lover's Complaint*
downstairs	an adverb meaning toward the lower floors	said by Prince Hal in *Henry IV, Part I*
drug	a verb meaning to add a toxic substance or narcotic to a food or drink	said by Lady Macbeth in *Macbeth*
elbow	a verb meaning to nudge or prod	said by Kent in *King Lear*
employer	a noun meaning a person who uses someone or something	said by Benedick in *Much Ado About Nothing*
exposure	a noun meaning the act of uncovering or leaving unprotected	said by Nestor in *Troilus and Cressida*
fancy-free	an adjective meaning free from the power of love	said by Oberon in *A Midsummer Night's Dream*
film	a verb meaning to coat or cover thinly	said by Hamlet in *Hamlet*
flawed	an adjective meaning weakened or damaged	said by Edgar in *King Lear*
fortune-teller	a noun meaning one who professes to predict the future	said by Antipholus of Ephesus in *The Comedy of Errors*
full-grown	an adjective meaning mature, fully developed	said by John Gower in *Pericles*
gloomy	an adjective meaning dark or shadowy	said by Joan la Pucell in *Henry VI, Part I*
gossip	a noun meaning someone given to loose talk about friends	said by the Abbess in *The Comedy of Errors*
green-eyed	an adjective meaning envious	said by Portia in *The Merchant of Venice*
homicide	a noun meaning killer	said by Reignier in *Henry VI, Part I*
hurry	a verb meaning move quickly	said by Adriana in *The Comedy of Errors*
ill-starred	an adjective meaning unfortunate	said by Othello in *Othello*

Word	Usage/Meaning	Shakespeare Connection
ill-tempered	an adjective meaning having a bad temper, unwholesome	said by Brutus in *Julius Caesar*
label	a verb meaning to brand	said by Olivia in *Twelfth Night*
laughable	an adjective meaning humorous	said by Salarino in *The Merchant of Venice*
lonely	an adjective meaning isolated	said by Coriolanus in *Coriolanus*
lower	a verb meaning to reduce in height or standing	said by Mark Antony in *Antony and Cleopatra*
luggage	a noun meaning possessions, baggage	said by Prince Hal in *Henry IV, Part I*
madcap	an adjective meaning zany, foolish	said by Maria in *Love's Labour's Lost*
majestic	an adjective meaning having dignity or grandeur	said by Cassius in *Julius Caesar*
manager	a noun meaning someone or something that controls	said by Don Armado in *Love's Labour's Lost*
marketable	an adjective meaning saleable, attractive	said by Celia in *As You Like It*
mimic	a noun meaning a double, lookalike	said by Puck in *A Midsummer Night's Dream*
mountaineer	a noun meaning people who live in mountains, hillbillies	said by Cloten in *Cymbeline*
noiseless	an adjective meaning silent	said by the King in *All's Well That Ends Well*
obscene	an adjective meaning repulsive, gross, indecent	said by Ferdinand in *Love's Labour's Lost*
ode	a noun meaning a type of poem	said by Dumaine in *Love's Labour's Lost*
outbreak	a noun meaning a sudden eruption	said by Polonius in *Hamlet*
partner	a verb meaning to link or join with another	said by Jachimo in *Cymbeline*
puke	a verb meaning to vomit	said by Jaques in *As You Like It*
quarrelsome	an adjective meaning contentious, likely to bicker	said by Grumio in *The Taming of the Shrew*
radiance	a noun meaning brilliance	said by Helena in *All's Well That Ends Well*

Word	Usage/Meaning	Shakespeare Connection
rant	a verb meaning to speak out loudly	said by Hamlet in *Hamlet*
retirement	a noun meaning the giving up of a position	said by the The Earl of Douglas in *Henry IV, Part I*
rival	an adjective meaning completing	said by Theseus in *A Midsummer Night's Dream*
scuffle	a noun meaning aggressive actions, fights	said by Philo in *Antony and Cleopatra*
secure	a verb meaning to make safe, to guarantee	said by Queen Margaret in *Henry VI, Part II*
shooting star	a noun meaning a meteor glowing from atmospheric friction	said by the Earl of Salisbury in *Richard II*
skim milk	a noun meaning milk with cream removed	said by Hotspur in *Henry IV, Part I*
soft-hearted	an adjective meaning sympathetic to a fault	said by Queen Margaret in *Henry VI, Part II*
submerge	a verb meaning put underwater	said by Cleopatra in *Antony and Cleopatra*
superscript	a noun meaning address	said by Holofernes in *Love's Labour's Lost*
swagger	a verb meaning to assume an attitude above one's station	said by Puck in *A Midsummer Night's Dream*
tardiness	a noun meaning lateness, slowness	said by the King of France in *King Lear*
torture	a verb meaning to hurt for a cause	said by Simpcox in *Henry VI, Part II*
tranquil	an adjective meaning quiet, temperate, still	said by Othello in *Othello*
unaware	an adverb meaning unknowingly, inadvertently	said by Venus in *Venus and Adonis*
unchanging	an adverb meaning not varying, always the same	said by York in *Henry VI, Part III*
undervalue	a verb meaning to give a lower rating or worth than justified	said by Bassanio in *The Merchant of Venice*
varied	an adjective meaning different, changing, showing different examples of something	said by Marcus in *Titus Andronicus*
well-behaved	an adjective meaning courteous, polite conduct	said by Mistress Ford in *The Merry Wives of Windsor*
wormhole	a noun meaning the burrow of a worm	said by Lucrece in *The Rape of Lucrece*

Word	Usage/Meaning	Shakespeare Connection
worthless	an adjective meaning without value	said by the Earl of Warwick in *Henry VI, Part III*
zany	a noun meaning a wild uncontrolled person, mimic, clown	said by Berowne in *Love's Labour's Lost*

Challenge

Word	Usage/Meaning	Shakespeare Connection
academe	a noun meaning a school or place of learning	said by Ferdinand in *Love's Labour's Lost*
addiction	a noun meaning habit	said by the Archbishop of Canterbury in *Henry V*
anchovy	a noun meaning small fish of the herring family	said by Peto in *Henry IV, Part I*
assassination	a noun meaning a planned murder	said by Macbeth in *Macbeth*
bedazzle	a verb meaning confuse with brilliance	said by Kate in *The Taming of the Shrew*
besmirch	a verb meaning to smear or stain	said by Laertes in *Hamlet*
castigate	a verb meaning to punish or rebuke severely	said by Apemantus in *Timon of Athens*
cater	a verb meaning to act as provider of food	said by Adam in *As You Like It*
cow	a verb meaning to intimidate, to frighten	said by Macduff in *Macbeth*
dauntless	an adjective meaning fearless	said by King Lewis XI in *Henry VI, Part III*
dickens	a noun meaning heck, devil	said by Mistress Page in *The Merry Wives of Windsor*
discontent	a noun meaning unhappiness, dissatisfaction	said by Saturninus in *Titus Andronicus*
engagement	a noun meaning commitment or pledge	said by Brutus in *Julius Caesar*
epileptic	an adjective meaning the condition of having epilepsy; to be jerky, uncontrolled	said by Kent in *King Lear*
fitful	an adjective meaning relating to a disease; troubled; disturbed	said by Macbeth in *Macbeth*

Word	Usage/Meaning	Shakespeare Connection
foppish	an adjective meaning foolish, silly	said by the Fool in *King Lear*
frugal	an adjective meaning not wasteful	said by Mistress Page in *The Merry Wives of Windsor*
gallantry	a noun meaning politeness, bravery	said by Paris in *Troilus and Cressida*
go-between	a noun meaning a messenger	said by Falstaff in *The Merry Wives of Windsor*
grovel	a verb meaning to kowtow, to humble oneself	said by Eleanor in *Henry VI, Part II*
hobnob	a verb (hob, nob) meaning to socialize with	said by Sir Toby Belch in *Twelfth Night*
humor	a verb meaning to satisfy, to indulge	said by Moth in *Love's Labour's Lost*
inauspicious	an adjective meaning ill-omened, unlucky	said by Romeo in *Romeo and Juliet*
invulnerable	an adjective meaning indestructible, not able to be hurt	said by King Philip in *King John*
jaded	an adjective meaning bored, disinterested	said by Suffolk in *Henry VI, Part II*
jet	a verb meaning to intrude	said by Aaron the Moor in *Titus Andronicus*
lackluster	an adjective meaning dull, mediocre	said by Jaques in *As You Like It*
lustrous	an adjective meaning shining, glossy	said by the Clown in *Twelfth Night*
metamorphose	a verb meaning to change	said by Proteus in *The Two Gentlemen of Verona*
negotiate	a verb meaning to bargain	said by Claudio in *Much Ado About Nothing*
obsequiously	an adverb meaning with deep respect and deference	said by Lady Anne in *Richard III*
pedant	a noun meaning teacher	said by Hortensio in *The Taming of the Shrew*
petition	a verb meaning to request	said by Mark Antony in *Antony and Cleopatra*
premeditated	an adjective meaning considered, planned	said by the Bishop of Winchester in *Henry VI, Part I*
remorseless	an adjective meaning without guilt or sympathy	said by King Henry VI in *Henry VI, Part II*

Word	Usage/Meaning	Shakespeare Connection
sacrificial	an adjective meaning worshipful, relating to a sacrifice or offering	said by the Poet in *Timon of Athens*
savagery	a noun meaning wild, violent behavior	said by Salisbury in *King John*
stealthy	an adjective meaning secretive, hidden	said by Macbeth in *Macbeth*
unearthly	an adjective meaning not of this planet	said by Dion in *The Winter's Tale*
unpublished	an adjective meaning secret, not issued	said by Cordelia in *King Lear*
unwillingness	a noun meaning the quality of being unwilling; disinclination	said by Richard in *Richard II*
vaulting	an adjective meaning soaring overarching	said by Queen Margaret in *Henry VI, Part II*
vulnerable	an adjective meaning open to harm	said by Macbeth in *Macbeth*

WORDS COINED FROM LITERATURE AND MOVIES

Just as many words from Shakespeare's works have become part of the English language, new words from literature and movies have also become part of the lexicon.

Easy

Word	Origin	Meaning
robot	coined by Karel Capek in *R.U.R.*	a machine programmed to carry out human-like tasks and activities
scrooge	Ebenezer Scrooge, a character in *A Christmas Carol by* Charles Dickens	an extremely stingy and miserly person
sherlock	Sherlock Holmes, the detective in Arthur Conan Doyle's mysteries	a detective

Target

Word	Origin	Meaning
Big Brother	George Orwell's *Nineteen Eighty-Four*	a dictator or a dictatorship that watches everything one does
broken-hearted	coined by William Tyndale, English translator of the Bible, in Luke 4:18	inconsolable; grief-stricken
Camelot	the site of King Arthur's legendary court	any ideal place
cantankerous	coined by Oliver Goldsmith in *She Stoops to Conquer*	cranky; bad-tempered
Catch-22	coined by Joseph Heller in the novel *Catch-22*	a situation or problem that can't be solved
doublethink	coined by George Orwell in *Nineteen Eighty-Four*	believing two contradictory things at the same time
eleventh hour	the Bible, Matthew 20:1-16	the latest possible time
elfin	coined by Edmund Spenser in *The Fairie Queene*	like an elf
fedora	Fedora Romanoff, a leading character in Victorien Sardou's play *Fedora*	a soft felt hat

Word	Origin	Meaning
freelance	coined by Sir Walter Scott in *Ivanhoe*	knights who sold their services to any master
good Samaritan	the Bible, Luke 10:30-85	a stranger who stops to help another
newspeak	coined by George Orwell in *Nineteen Eighty-Four*	language used to mislead the public
pollyanna	the main character in M. Porter's novel *Pollyanna*	someone who is foolishly optimistic
Shangri-la	coined by James Hilton in *Lost Horizon*	a paradise on Earth
underdog	a popular 19th-century song by David Barker called "The Under-Dog in the Fight"	a person expected to lose

Challenge

Word	Origin	Meaning
braggadocio	coined by Edmund Spenser in *The Fairie Queene*	a braggart; excessive boasting
dust devil	coined by F.M. Parker in *Skinner*	a small dust storm or whirlwind
gargantuan	originally a character from French folktales but made popular by François Rabelais in *Gargantua and Pantagruel*	enormous; gigantic
jeremiad	Jeremiah, a Hebrew prophet from the Old Testament	a long mournful tale of trouble and woe
lilliputian	the Lilliputians in Jonathan Swift's *Gulliver's Travels*	tiny; little; of no importance
malapropism	Mrs. Malaprop in Richard Sheridan's *The Rivals*	a mistake in which one important-sounding word is confused with another
pandemonium	coined by John Milton in *Paradise Lost*	chaos
paparazzi	Signore Paparazzo, a photographer in Federico Fellini's film *La Dolce Vita*	a freelance photographer of celebrities
quixotic	coined by Miguel de Cervantes in *Don Quixote de la Mancha*	having an over romantic view of life; lofty-minded and impractical
replicant	Ridley Scott's movie *Blade Runner*	an android; a bioengineered being
thought police	George Orwell's *Nineteen Eighty-Four*	people who control or try to control what others think

Chapter 3

Words From Other Languages

> "*We're studying the influence of other languages on English. I need some examples of English words that come from many different languages, not just from Spanish and French.*"

This chapter explores the history of English by focusing on words and phrases derived from other languages. More than twenty languages are represented in the lists that follow, enriching students' knowledge of their influence on English. While some of the words have changed in spelling and/or pronunciation as they have been adopted into English, students may notice that others have remained in their original form.

Because we use Latin and Greek roots to build words, the English language owes a great debt to these two languages. In addition, many Latin words in particular have passed into English through several other languages. Share with students the following example from *Building Your Vocabulary* (Scholastic, 2002):

> The English word *delicatessen* came from
> a German word, *delikatessen*, which came from
> a French word, *délicatesse*, which came from
> a Latin word, *delicatus*, which means "pleasing."

The Greek and Latin words included in the lists in this chapter are either ones that appear pretty much as they do in their original language or ones that can be traced more directly back to the original language. You may wish to show students the word origin information that is typically included in a dictionary entry so that they can continue to study word origins on their own.

WORDS FROM AFRICAN LANGUAGES

Easy

Word	Meaning	Word	Meaning
banana	a fruit	yam	a vegetable
cola	a drink		

Target

Word	Meaning	Word	Meaning
aardvark	a mammal with a long snout	safari	a hunting trip or trip to see animals
dashiki	a brightly colored, loose-fitting garment	samba	a dance
gumbo	a thick, spicy stew	zombie	the living dead
marimba	a dance		

Challenge

Word	Meaning	Word	Meaning
apartheid	a system of racial segregation	raffia	a type of fiber made from leaves
dengue	an infectious disease	veld	grassland
kraal	a rural village		

WORDS FROM ARABIC

Easy

Word	Meaning	Word	Meaning
ghoul	a ghost or phantom	sofa	a couch
magazine	a weekly or monthly publication	zero	nothing
mummy	an embalmed body wrapped in cloth		

Target

Word	Meaning
admiral	a commander
algebra	a field in mathematics
alcohol	a fermented beverage
assassin	killer, especially of an important person
falafel	fried balls of ground, spiced chickpeas
hummus	a dip of mashed chickpeas
jinni	a spirit
kebab	grilled meat and vegetables on a stick

Word	Meaning
kohl	a dark powder often used as eyeliner
loofah	a type of sponge
mecca	a place thought to be a center of activity
monsoon	a torrential rainstorm
sheik	the leader of an Arab tribe
sultan	a ruler
tariff	a tax on imported and sometimes exported goods

Challenge

Word	Meaning
caliph	a Muslim ruler
casbah	the older section of a North African town
dhow	a one- or two-masted sailing ship
elixir	a sweetened drink or potion
emir	a ruler
fakir	a holy man who lives by begging

Word	Meaning
fatwa	a religious decree
hegira	a flight or escape
kismet	fate
intifada	an uprising
jihad	a military campaign or holy war
mufti	civilian clothes worn by a military person

WORDS FROM AUSTRALIAN

Easy

Word	Meaning
kangaroo	a mammal with a pouch

Word	Meaning
koala	an animal resembling a small bear

Target

Word	Meaning
boomerang	a weapon made from a curved piece of wood

Word	Meaning
dingo	a wild dog

Challenge

Word	Meaning		Word	Meaning
billabong	a water hole		didgeridoo	a musical instrument

WORDS FROM CHINESE

Easy

Word	Meaning		Word	Meaning
china	tableware made of porcelain		tea	a drink made from dried leaves
chop suey	vegetable dish with fish or meat		wok	a metal pan for stir-frying
chow mein	fried noodle dish with shredded meat		wonton	a dumpling
ketsup	a spicy, tomato-based sauce			

Target

Word	Meaning		Word	Meaning
dim sum	small portions of various dishes		mahjong	a type of board game
ginseng	a root often used in Chinese medicine		mandarin	the highest-ranked public official
gung ho	very eager and excited		soy	sauce made from beans
kowtow	kneel and touch head to floor; to fawn over		tofu	bean curd
kumquat	a small citrus fruit		typhoon	a violent windstorm
kung fu	a martial art used for self-defense		yang	sun; masculine principle
			yin	moon; feminine principle

Challenge

Word	Meaning		Word	Meaning
feng shui	system of beliefs about people's relationship with the environment		tai chi	a form of physical exercise and meditation
sampan	a flat-bottomed boat		tao	the way or guiding principle

WORDS FROM DUTCH

Easy

Word	Meaning	Word	Meaning
cookie	a little, flat cake	snoop	to pry or spy
skate	to glide across ice	stove	an appliance on which one cooks
sled	a small vehicle with runners for moving over ice and snow	tulip	a flower
sleigh	an open vehicle with runners pulled by a horse over ice or snow	waffle	a type of pancake
		walrus	a sea mammal
snack	a between-meals treat	wiggle	twist and jiggle

Target

Word	Meaning	Word	Meaning
bluff	to pretend or fake	knack	a special talent or clever way of doing something
coleslaw	a salad of sliced cabbage	pickle	a cucumber that has been soaked in brine
cruise	a voyage by water		
cruller	a small cake of fried dough	splinter	a small, thin piece of wood
decoy	a lure or snare	stoop	a small porch or staircase
duffel	a type of woolen material; a bag	yacht	a type of boat
easel	a device for holding a painter's canvas		

Challenge

Word	Meaning	Word	Meaning
maelstrom	a violent whirlpool	schooner	a fast sailing ship
mannequin	a life-size dummy	scone	a small cake of baked bread
mart	a store	sloop	a single-masted ship
roster	a list	smelt	to melt or fuse in order to produce metal

WORDS FROM FRENCH

Easy

Word	Meaning	Word	Meaning
ballet	a type of dance	menu	a list of food items being served
beret	a soft, flat hat	omelette	an egg dish
cafe	a place that serves coffee	picnic	a casual meal eaten outside, often sitting on the grass
chauffeur	someone who drives someone else's car	portrait	a picture of a person
corduroy	a type of ribbed fabric	restaurant	a place that serves food
coupon	a piece of paper giving the bearer certain benefits, such as a discount	masquerade	a party at which masks and costumes are worn
crayon	a colored stick, often of wax, used for drawing	touché	word used to show a person has scored or made a point
margarine	food product usually made from vegetable oils	unique	one of a kind
mayonnaise	a beaten mixture of oil and egg white		

Target

Word	Meaning	Word	Meaning
ambiance	atmosphere or mood of a place	crochet	a type of needlework done with a hooked needle
arabesque	a type of dance position	croquet	a game played on grass
attaché	a military or governmental agent; a civil servant	croquette	a small meat or potato ball coated with bread crumbs
bayonet	a steel blade attached at the muzzle of a gun	crouton	a small piece of dried bread
bayou	marshland; swampland	cuisine	style of cooking
bistro	a small, informal restaurant	debris	remains; rubbish
cabaret	a nightclub or restaurant where people can enjoy a floor-show	debut	first appearance
cache	a hidden store of things	detour	a bypass or route taken around something
camouflage	to disguise or conceal	diplomat	an ambassador
casserole	a type of stew	encore	a repeated performance or part of it that is repeated
cassette	a plastic cartridge containing magnetic tape	etiquette	a system of appropriate behavior
coupé	a small, two-doored car	fiancé	a man engaged to be married
courier	a messenger	fiancée	a woman engaged to be married

Word	Meaning
gaffe	a noticeable mistake; blunder
gourmet	a person with knowledge and love of good food
marinade	a sauce for soaking meat before cooking
mauve	a light purple color
memoir	a personal account of one's life
mortgage	a type of written agreement for borrowing money for property
mutiny	rebellion against legal authority
naïve	inexperienced and too trusting
née	born
passé	out of date
plaque	a sign or tablet
potpourri	a mixture of flowers and herbs
promenade	walk
protégé	a young person who receives guidance from an older person

Word	Meaning
publicity	advertising
queue	line
quiche	a pie made with a filling of eggs and cream
ratchet	a tool
repertoire	a body of work that can be performed
reservoir	an artificial lake
résumé	summary of education, experience, and qualifications
revenue	income from business
sauté	cooked quickly in butter or oil
soufflé	a light baked dish made with egg whites
souvenir	a memento or reminder of a particular place or event
vogue	fashion; trend
zest	flavor; enthusiasm; enjoyment for life

Challenge

Word	Meaning
abattoir	a place where animals are slaughtered
accoutrements	accessories; clothing or equipment
adroit	skillful
apropos	appropriate for a particular situation
avant-garde	ultra-modern
blasé	unimpressed
bourgeois	middle-class; conventional, materialistic, and boring
cul-de-sac	a dead end
dossier	bundle of papers relating to a particular topic
echelon	rank or level

Word	Meaning
entourage	followers or associates
entrepreneur	someone who sets up his/her own business to make money
envoy	someone acting as a messenger for another country
espionage	spying
finesse	skill; flair
gauche	awkward; vulgar
impromptu	without preparation
insouciance	lack of concern; calm and untroubled manner
intrigue	plot or scheme
liaison	a person who links or coordinates others
macabre	suggesting death; gruesome; chilling

Word	Meaning	Word	Meaning
maladroit	clumsy; awkward	rapport	bond of understanding
nuance	a very slight difference	regime	government in power
nonchalant	casual; calm and unconcerned	renaissance	rebirth of culture
panache	style and self-confidence	rendezvous	meeting
piquant	spicy	ricochet	to rebound or bounce back
raconteur	a storyteller	sabotage	subversive, destructive act
repartee	witty banter	sachet	a little package of scent

WORDS FROM GERMAN

Easy

Word	Meaning	Word	Meaning
dachshund	a type of dog with a long body	knapsack	a backpack
delicatessen	a shop selling prepared cooked meats, relishes, cheeses, etc.	noodle	a strip of pasta
dollar	100 cents; a unit of money	polka	a type of fast dance
frankfurter	a hotdog	pretzel	a crisp bakery product usually shaped like a knot
hamster	a small domesticated rodent		
hamburger	a patty of chopped meat	pumpernickel	a coarse, dark bread
kindergarten	a school for young children or grade before first grade	wiener	a hot dog
		yodel	a type of singing

Target

Word	Meaning	Word	Meaning
blitz	heavy and swift air bombardment	gesundheit	a kind of blessing or wish when someone sneezes
bratwurst	a sausage made of spiced pork or veal	glitz	glamour; glitter
edelweiss	a European alpine plant	glockenspiel	a percussion instrument
foosball	a table game	kaiser	emperor or ruler
flugelhorn	a musical instrument	kaput	broken; ruined
frau	a married woman	kitsch	tacky or lowbrow
fräulein	a young or unmarried woman	knockwurst	short, thick sausage
gestapo	secret police	liverwurst	a liver sausage

Word	Meaning
linzer torte	a type of cake with fruit
loden	a thick, dark-green woolen cloth
Luftwaffe	German air force
plunder	to take property by force
poltergeist	a noisy and mischievous ghost
rottweiler	a breed of dog
rucksack	a backpack
sauerkraut	a dish of shredded, sour cabbage
schnauzer	a type of rough-haired terrier
schwa	an unstressed vowel sound
shyster	an unscrupulous or contemptible person, coward

Word	Meaning
schmooze	to meet and talk informally
snorkel	a breathing tube used for diving
spritz	squirt or spray
stein	a large beer mug
streusel	a pastry with a sweet crumbly topping
torte	a rich cake made with eggs and ground nuts
waltz	a type of dance or dance music
wurst	a sausage
zwieback	a type of bread that is baked and then toasted

Challenge

Word	Meaning
angst	anxiety and worry
cobalt	a metallic element
doppelgänger	a double
ersatz	fake or imitation
feldspar	a metamorphic rock
fest	a get-together or celebration
flak	bursting or shells from artillery
gestalt	big or total picture; the whole form
gneiss	a rock resembling granite
hinterland	backcountry, remote region
howitzer	cannon with medium-length barrel
lebensraum	territory needed for a country to expand

Word	Meaning
lederhosen	knee-length leather trousers
leitmotif	a recurring theme
meerschaum	a tobacco pipe
muesli	a cereal of untoasted, rolled oats, nuts and dried fruit
panzer	an armored vehicle such as a tank
Reich	German empire
spiel	extravagant talk; a sales pitch
umlaut	a diacritical mark
verboten	forbidden
wanderlust	a longing to travel
wunderkind	an extremely talented child
zeitgeist	spirit of the time

WORDS FROM GREEK

Easy

Word	Meaning	Word	Meaning
alphabet	the letters in a language	hippopotamus	a large mammal that lives in rivers
buffalo	a type of cattle with horns	rhinoceros	a large mammal with one or two horns on its nose
chorus	a group of singers	rhythm	beat
church	a place of worship		
crocodile	a large reptile		

Target

Word	Meaning	Word	Meaning
academy	a school	horizon	point where the sky seems to touch the earth
acoustic	relating to sound	marathon	a foot race of about 26 miles
agony	struggle and pain	mathematics	the study of numbers and how they work
amnesia	the inability to remember one's past	meander	to wander
amoeba	a one-celled organism	mechanic	a person who repairs machines
athlete	someone who plays sports and other physical activities	melody	rhythmically organized tones that create a musical quality
catastrophe	a disaster	metropolis	a city
ceramic	a mixture of clay and chemicals	mime	a type of performance in which characters are portrayed through physical movements
chaos	complete disorder		
character	a person in a story		
democracy	government by the people	mystery	something difficult to understand
dinosaur	a prehistoric and extinct reptile	prophet	a seer
drama	a serious play	psalm	a hymn or song of praise
economy	management of resources	sympathy	understanding and compassion
epitaph	an inscription, particularly one on a tombstone	tragedy	a drama that ends unhappily or in which the main character is brought to ruin
gymnasium	a place equipped for sports		
history	the story of the past		

Challenge

Word	Meaning
abyss	an extremely deep chasm; a void
acme	the peak or perfection
agora	marketplace
allegory	the use of characters to represent ideas
alpha	the beginning
anathema	something that is reviled
anarchy	chaos and disorder
aristocracy	members of the noble class
asbestos	a type of heat-resistance mineral
cosmos	the ordered universe
dogma	doctrine
epiphany	a revelation

Word	Meaning
holocaust	massive slaughter of people
martyr	a person who suffers willingly for a cause
melancholy	sadness
myriad	a multitude
obelisk	a large stone that serves as a monument
omega	the end
ostracize	to exclude
sarcasm	mockery
stigma	a mark of shame or disgrace
syntax	the pattern or rules of a language
thesis	a proposition

WORDS FROM HINDI

Easy

Word	Meaning
bangle	a bracelet
bandanna	a scarf
cot	a folding bed

Word	Meaning
pajamas	sleeping attire
shampoo	a cleanser for hair

Target

Word	Meaning
bungalow	a simple one-storied house or cottage
calico	a patterned, coarse cotton cloth
chintz	a brightly colored, printed, glazed fabric
dinghy	a small boat

Word	Meaning
dungarees	jeans
khaki	a dull brownish-yellow color
loot	plunder
swami	a religious leader
thug	a brutal person
veranda	a porch

Challenge

Word	Meaning	Word	Meaning
chutney	a relish	maharani	a Hindu princess
cummerbund	a pleated sash worn for formal dress	pundit	a critic
jodhpurs	riding breeches	swami	a religious teacher
juggernaut	a relentlessly destructive force	tandoori	a dish cooked in a clay oven over charcoal
maharaja	a Hindu prince		

WORDS FROM ITALIAN

Easy

Word	Meaning	Word	Meaning
bandit	an outlaw; a thief	pizza	flat bread with cheese and sauce
broccoli	a green vegetable	solo	alone
macaroni	a type of pasta	spaghetti	a type of pasta
motto	a statement expressing goals	violin	a stringed instrument
pasta	noodles made from flour, eggs, and water	volcano	an opening from which molten rock erupts from the earth
piano	a large musical instrument with a keyboard		

Target

Word	Meaning	Word	Meaning
balcony	a terrace	graffiti	writings and drawings made on walls
ballot	a system of voting	grotto	a cave
bravo	excellent; well-done	influenza	a respiratory disease
casino	a public place for gambling	lava	molten rock from a volcano
confetti	streamers of colored paper	maestro	a master
fiasco	total failure	malaria	a disease transmitted by mosquitoes
finale	the end		
ghetto	a segregated area of a city	mandolin	a stringed instrument
gondola	a long, narrow boat		

Word	Meaning	Word	Meaning
marina	a harbor; a place where boats are docked	soprano	a singer with a high voice
mezzanine	a floor midway between the first and second floors	studio	a workroom for an artist
		torso	the trunk of the body
opera	a dramatic work that is sung	zany	comical

Challenge

Word	Meaning	Word	Meaning
a cappella	singing without musical accompaniment	libretto	the text for an opera
alfresco	in the open air	madrigal	a song
allegro	quick and lively	paparazzi	photographers who pursue celebrities
antipasto	appetizer	portfolio	a flat case for holding papers
aria	a melody that is sung by one person alone or two people together	regatta	a boat race
cappuccino	coffee with hot milk	sonata	a type of classical music
concerto	a musical composition	staccato	short, rapid notes
crescendo	a gradual increase in the volume of music	stiletto	a dagger
		stucco	a plaster coating used for outer walls
diva	an important woman singer, especially one who is arrogant	svelte	slender
		trattoria	a small, simple restaurant or tavern
fascism	a system of government headed by a dictator	vendetta	a feud
incognito	disguised	virtuoso	an expert or particularly skillful person

WORDS FROM JAPANESE

Easy

Word	Meaning	Word	Meaning
haiku	a poem of three lines with a total of 17 syllables	karate	a martial art that uses kicks and punches
judo	a martial art similar to wrestling		

Target

Word	Meaning	Word	Meaning
banzai	a Japanese battle cry	sake	an alcoholic beverage made from rice
bonsai	a miniaturized tree or shrub	samurai	a warrior
futon	a sleeping mat	sashimi	thin slices of raw fish
hibachi	a grill	sushi	raw fish and rice
honcho	the person in charge	tofu	a food made from bean curd
jujitsu	a martial art that relies on wrestling techniques	tsunami	a giant wave caused by an underground earthquake
manga	a style of comic or graphic book	tycoon	a powerful business magnate
ninja	a fighter trained as an assassin		
origami	the art of paper folding		

Challenge

Word	Meaning	Word	Meaning
aikido	a martial art	shogun	a ruler
kabuki	a form of drama	shiatsu	a type of massage
karaoke	entertainment where a person sings along with a prerecorded song	sumo	a type of wrestler
		tatami	a straw mat
nisei	an American whose parents came from Japan		

WORDS FROM LATIN

Easy

Word	Meaning	Word	Meaning
alibi	excuse or explanation	pro	for
arena	enclosed area for a sporting event	quota	allowed amount
exit	way out	recipe	instructions for preparing food
index	a listing showing topics	rex	king
minus	reduced by	versus	against; opposed to

BF 637 S4 R592 2009

Due: 08/14/2010 : 11:59
PM
Returned: 07/12/2010 :
01:19 PM

FINE: +0.00

CHECKIN
McEnery,TreeAnne

39080021107923
Applying to graduate
school in psychology :

University Library

BF 77 A67 2008

Due: 08/14/2010 : 11:59
PM
Returned: 07/12/2010 :
01:18 PM

FINE: +0.00

Target

Word	Meaning
alias	assumed name
ante	bet; to put up in advance
apex	highest point
cursor	pointer
data	information
focus	concentrate attention on
forum	a place or opportunity for meeting and discussing
fungus	a type of organism
habitat	environment
media	mass communication
memento	souvenir
memorabilia	things that help you remember a person or event
memorandum	a brief communication
minutia	little details
nil	nothing
opus	work
par	standard or average
pleb	common person
re	regarding
sic	thus; so
sinister	evil; wicked
stet	keep or restore
subpoena	an order for someone to appear in court
thesaurus	a collection of synonyms and sometimes antonyms
veto	vote against
via	by way of

Challenge

Word	Meaning
acumen	keenness of judgment
addendum	something added
affidavit	sworn statement
anima	spirit; inner self
atrium	entrance hall
auspices	guidance; protection
cadaver	dead body
caveat	warning; caution
credo	belief
crux	heart of the matter
decorum	good manners
dementia	a disease that causes mental deterioration
ergo	therefore
erratum	error
exemplar	example
fiat	formal authorization
genus	the ranking between species and family
gratis	free
gravitas	seriousness
honorarium	money paid to someone who gives a speech
hiatus	pause; break
impetus	drive; momentum
inertia	inactivity
juvenalia	work done when a writer or artist was young
limbo	dividing line

Word	Meaning		Word	Meaning
lacuna	a gap; something missing		persona	character or assumed role
matrix	the situation from which something originates		placebo	drug without any active ingredients, used in a test situation
modicum	small amount		stratum	level
mores	customs and habits		tenet	principle
nexus	connection or link		verbatim	exactly as said

WORDS FROM NATIVE AMERICAN LANGUAGES

Easy

Word	Meaning		Word	Meaning
chipmunk	a small striped rodent		papoose	a young child or baby
igloo	a dwelling made of packed snow		tomahawk	a small weapon with a sharp blade
moccasin	a type of soft shoe made of leather		wampum	polished beads used for money
parka	a hooded jacket		wigwam	a type of hut

Target

Word	Meaning		Word	Meaning
hickory	a type of tree		succotash	a dish made of corn and lima beans
husky	a breed of dog used to pull sleds		toboggan	a narrow sled without runners
kayak	a lightweight canoe		totem	a carving representing an animal or object important to a tribe
pecan	a type of edible nut			
squash	a vegetable			

Challenge

Word	Meaning		Word	Meaning
anorak	a long jacket with a hood		wickiup	a type of hut

WORDS FROM PORTUGUESE

Easy

Word	Meaning	Word	Meaning
samba	a dance	zebra	a wild animal similar to a horse that has black and white stripes on its body

Target

Word	Meaning	Word	Meaning
commando	a military unit that conducts dangerous raids	pagoda	a Buddhist temple

Challenge

Word	Meaning	Word	Meaning
junta	military rule	peon	a farmworker or menial worker
mangrove	a type of tree or shrub	tapioca	a starch from the root of the cassava plant

WORDS FROM RUSSIAN

Easy

Word	Meaning	Word	Meaning
czar	a Russian ruler	sputnik	an artificial satellite
sable	an animal prized for its fur		

Target

Word	Meaning	Word	Meaning
babushka	a head scarf	cosmonaut	a Russian astronaut
blintz	a thin pancake	cossack	a peasant
borscht	a soup made from beets	kremlin	a Russian citadel or fortress

Word	Meaning		Word	Meaning
mammoth	a hairy, extinct elephant		tundra	permanently frozen, treeless land
shaman	a sage or spiritualist		yurt	a tent
steppe	prairieland			

Challenge

Word	Meaning		Word	Meaning
glasnost	a policy of openness and cooperation		politburo	the executive branch of the Communist government
gulag	a labor camp		samovar	a tea urn
perestroika	a restructuring of government		troika	a carriage drawn by three horses
pogrom	an officially sanctioned system of persecution			

WORDS FROM SANSKRIT

Easy

Word	Meaning		Word	Meaning
om	a sacred syllable used in prayers and chants		yoga	a discipline or system that includes breathing exercises and postures

Target

Word	Meaning		Word	Meaning
karma	fate		nirvana	a state of enlightenment; paradise
mandala	a circular design representing the universe mantra		yogi	a person who practices yoga

Challenge

Word	Meaning	Word	Meaning
ashram	a retreat	raga	a form of music
avatar	someone who embodies certain principles or a figure that represents a person	swastika	a religious symbol that later became a fascist symbol
dharma	duty or truth	tantra	sacred books

WORDS FROM SCANDINAVIAN LANGUAGES

Easy

Word	Meaning	Word	Meaning
flounder	a type of flatfish	ski	a sport in which people glide down mountains on narrow strips of wood, metal, or plastic
mink	an animal prized for its fur		

Target

Word	Meaning	Word	Meaning
slalom	a downhill ski race	wicker	material woven from twigs or weeds
smorgasbord	a buffet		

Challenge

Word	Meaning	Word	Meaning
fjord	a long, narrow body of water surrounded by steep cliffs	ombudsman	a government official responsible for investigating complaints
gauntlet	a protective glove	tungsten	a metallic element
krill	tiny creatures that are eaten by baleen whales and other marine animals	gravlax	thin slices of cured salmon
		lingonberry	a type of red berry

WORDS FROM SPANISH

Easy

Word	Meaning	Word	Meaning
adios	good-bye	flamingo	a long-legged pink bird
alligator	a large reptile with sharp teeth	guitar	a stringed instrument
amigo	a friend	hombre	man
barrio	a section of a city where Spanish-speaking people live	hurricane	a violent wind storm
		mosquito	an insect
bronco	a wild horse	patio	an outdoor living area
burrito	a tortilla wrapped around a filling	potato	a white tuber cooked as a vegetable
burro	a small donkey		
breeze	a gentle wind	ranch	a farm where livestock are raised
chili	a pod of the pepper plant	salsa	a spicy sauce
chocolate	a sweet treat made from cocoa butter and milk	siesta	an afternoon nap
		sombrero	a hat
cigar	a roll of tobacco leaves	taco	a tortilla with filling
cockroach	an insect that is a household pest	tamale	fried meats and vegetables in a corn husk
coyote	an animal that is somewhat similar to a wolf		
		tobacco	dried leaves that are smoked
fajita	strips of meat served on a soft tortilla	tomato	a type of fruit often used in salads
fiesta	a celebration	tortilla	thin, flat bread

Target

Word	Meaning	Word	Meaning
adobe	a brick made from straw and earth	cafeteria	a coffee shop or informal restaurant
armadillo	an animal with hard plates covering its body	cantina	an eating place that also sells liquor
armada	a large fleet of ships		
arroyo	a gulch or gorge	cannibal	a person who eats other humans
avocado	a type of fruit	canyon	a valley with a river running through it bordered by steep cliffs
barracuda	a predatory fish		
bodega	a grocery store	cargo	freight
bravado	boldness; display of courage	corral	a fenced area for livestock
buckaroo	a cowboy	crimson	deep red

Word	Meaning	Word	Meaning
desperado	a desperate outlaw	pampas	grass-covered plains
flotilla	a fleet of ships	papaya	a tropical fruit
galleon	a large sailing ship with three masts	plaza	a public square
gaucho	a cowboy	poncho	an outer garment or blanket with a slit for the head that is worn over the shoulders
guacamole	a dish made from mashed avocados		
hacienda	a large farm or ranch	puma	a mountain lion
hammock	a hanging bed made of ropes	quesadilla	a fried tortilla stuffed with cheese
iguana	a tropical lizard	rodeo	a competition with bronco riding and cattle roping
jaguar	a large cat similar to a leopard		
jalapeño	a type of spicy chili	rumba	a type of dance
jerky	dried meat	savanna	plains
lariat	a rope used to catch and tie up livestock	silo	a barn or cylinder used to store grain or animal feed
lasso	a rope used to catch livestock	stampede	headlong rush of animals
matador	a bullfighter	tango	a type of dance
mesa	flat, tableland	toreador	a bullfighter who fights on horseback
mustang	a wild horse		
nada	nothing	tornado	a destructive wind storm
oregano	a spice	vanilla	a flavoring
		vamoose	to leave in a hurry

Challenge

Word	Meaning	Word	Meaning
abalone	a marine creature with a pearly shell	guerrilla	a soldier who takes part in irregular warfare
aficionado	a fan	machete	a knife with a broad blade
albino	someone whose skin and hair lack pigmentation	machismo	exaggerated masculinity
		mariachi	a type of street band
cabana	a changing room or bath house	palmetto	a type of palm
condor	a large vulture	peccadillo	a small mistake or offense
conquistador	a Spanish conqueror	pimiento	a type of sweet red pepper
embarcadero	a pier or a boat dock	platinum	a precious metal that is silver-white
fandango	a type of dance		
guano	dung; bird or bat droppings	renegade	an outlaw
guava	a pear-shaped fruit		

WORDS FROM TURKISH

Easy

Word	Meaning	Word	Meaning
coffee	a hot beverage	sherbet	a frozen dessert made from fruit
fez	a brimless hat	yogurt	a type of fermented milk product

Target

Word	Meaning	Word	Meaning
bulgur	grain; dried cracked wheat	kiosk	a stall or booth
caftan	a loose-fitting robe	kismet	fate
divan	a sofa	minaret	a slender tower
harem	private quarters for women	mullah	a scholar or teacher
khan	a ruler	shish kebab	meat and vegetables on a skewer

Challenge

Word	Meaning	Word	Meaning
baklava	a dessert	janissary	a soldier or member of an elite group of supporters
dervish	a member of a religious order noted for its devotional dancing		

WORDS FROM YIDDISH

Easy

Word	Meaning	Word	Meaning
bagel	a bread roll shaped in a ring	matzo	unleavened bread

Target

Word	Meaning	Word	Meaning
klutz	a clumsy person	maven	an expert
knish	a seasoned potato cake	nosh	snack
kosher	following specific religious rules for preparing and selling food	pastrami	smoked, seasoned beef
		schnozzle	nose
kvetch	complain	yarmulke	a skull cap

Challenge

Word	Meaning	Word	Meaning
chutzpah	self-confidence; bravado	nebbish	a weak and timid person
golem	a clay creature brought to life	schlepp	to drag or carry
kaddish	a prayer for the dead	shtick	act or routine
mensch	a decent and honorable person	tchotchke	knick-knack, trinket

FRENCH PHRASES

Easy

Phrase	Meaning	Phrase	Meaning
à la carte	from a menu that prices each item separately	déjà vu	the feeling of having seen or done something before
à la mode	topped with ice cream	nom de plume	pen name
au gratin	with melted cheese		

Target

Phrase	Meaning	Phrase	Meaning
bon appétit	good appetite; enjoy the meal	femme fatale	a very attractive woman who breaks many men's hearts
bon vivant	a person who enjoys life and lives with style	hors d'oeuvre	an appetizer served before the main meal
carte blanche	license to do whatever one wants without consequences	in lieu of	instead of
double entendre	a remark with a double meaning	nouveau riche	people who have become rich recently
en route	on the road	tour de force	masterful work or skill
esprit de corps	team spirit		

Challenge

Word	Meaning	Word	Meaning
au pair	live-in domestic helper	faux pas	false step; embarrassing social mistake or blunder
bon mot	a witty remark	fin de siècle	end of the century
cause célèbre	a famous or notorious case or cause	joie de vivre	joy of life; enthusiasm
coup de grâce	stroke of kindness	laissez-faire	little control on free enterprise
coup d'état	the taking of power by force, as in military coup	noblesse oblige	rights and responsibilities coming from being high born
de rigueur	required or necessary	nouveau riche	people who have become rich recently
enfant terrible	a prodigy or remarkable person	par excellence	the very best
en masse	as a whole; all together	pièce de résistance	the best part of something
fait accompli	something already done or accomplished		

Word	Meaning	Word	Meaning
raison d'être	reason for being; justification	tête-à-tête	face-to-face or private conversation
savoir faire	confidence; flair in social situations		

LATIN PHRASES

Easy

Phrase	Meaning	Phrase	Meaning
et cetera (etc.)	and other things	per diem	by the day
ex libris	from the library	vice versa	the opposite; the other way around
in toto	completely		

Target

Phrase	Meaning	Phrase	Meaning
ad hoc	formed for a specific occasion or situation	mea culpa	the blame is mine
ad nauseum	to the point of nausea; sickening	nota bene	note well
bona fide	in good faith	per capita	per each head; per person
carpe diem	seize the day	persona non grata	a person who isn't welcome; someone unacceptable
cum laude	with honors	postmortem	after death
e pluribus unum	from many, one	pro bono	for the public good
ex post facto	done after the fact	summa cum laude	with highest honors
habeas corpus	you must have the body	tempus fugit	time flies
in media res	in the middle of things	terra firma	firm land; solid ground
magna cum laude	with high honors		

Challenge

Phrase	Meaning	Phrase	Meaning
ad hominem	appealing to personal considerations	in vitro	in glass; in an artificial environment
ad infinitum	with no limit	ipso facto	by that very fact
alma mater	school you formerly attended	lingua franca	language used by most people; commonly used language
a priori	conceived beforehand; self-evident	modus operandi	way of working
alter ego	other self; close friend	quid pro quo	this for that
caveat emptor	let the buyer beware	non sequitur	it does not follow
de facto	in fact	rara avis	rare bird; something rarely encountered
deus ex machina	a contrived solution or ending	tabula rasa	a blank slate
et alia (et al.)	and other things	terra incognita	unknown or unexplored land
in absentia	in the absence of		

SPANISH-ENGLISH COGNATES

Spanish-English cognates share the same Latin root. They look and sound very similar. In fact, in some cases, they are identical. Knowing cognates is a useful strategy for learning a new language.

Easy

Spanish Word	English Word	Spanish Word	English Word
acto	act	forma	form; shape
actor	actor	gas	gas
actriz	actress	gigante	giant
aire	air	globo	globe
altar	altar	honor	honor
banco	bank	hospital	hospital
banda	band	horrible	horrible
bandido	bandit	idea	idea
barra	bar	letra	letter
blusa	blouse	línea	line
bota	boot	lista	list
bote	boat	mapa	map
capa	cape	marcha	mark
capital	capital	natural	natural
capitán	captain	número	number
copia	copy	océano	ocean
correcto	correct	palma	palm
danza	dancing	pasta	paste; pasta; dough
eco	echo	patio	patio
error	error	perla	pearl
falso	false	rancho	ranch
fama	fame	té	tea
familia	family	tren	train
flor	flower		

Target

Spanish Word	English Word	Spanish Word	English Word
abnormal	abnormal	cuestión	question
abrupto	abrupt; steep	cupón	coupon
absorber	absorb	debatir	debate
academia	academy	decidir	decide
accidente	accident	decisión	decision
acento	accent	decorar	decorate
aceptar	accept	diferencia	difference
activo	active	dirección	direction
acusar	accuse	efecto	effect
adaptar	adapt	elegante	elegant
adjustar	adjust	elevar	elevate; raise
admitir	admit	emigrante	emigrant
adoptar	adopt	emoción	emotion
atleta	athlete	energía	energy
atención	attention	ensalada	salad
atractivo	attractive	eterno	enternal
audiencia	audience	fabuloso	fabulous
autobús	bus	famoso	famous
autor	author	favorable	favorable
avenida	avenue	festivo	festive; merry
balcón	balcony	generoso	generous
balón	ball	glorioso	glorious
banquero	banker	gratitud	gratitude
bicicleta	bicycle	hábito	habit; custom
biografía	biography	historia	history
border	border	honoria	honorary
calendario	calendar	humano	human being
candidato	candidate	identidad	identity
clínica	clinic	ilusión	illusion
combinar	combine	imperfecto	imperfect
convicto	convicted	importante	important
crear	create	imposible	impossible
cuarto	quarter	industria	industry
curioso	curious	información	information

Spanish Word	English Word	Spanish Word	English Word
lapso	lapse; mistake	opinión	opinion
lección	lesson	palacio	palace
libertad	liberty	pasado	past
lustre	luster; shine	permiso	permission
magnifico	magnificent	plantar	plant
magnitud	magnitude	policia	police
manual	manual; by hand	religión	religion
manuscrito	manuscript	satisfactorio	satisfactory
máximo	maximum	secreto	secret
medicina	medicine	selección	selection
memoria	memory	teatro	theater
mérito	merit; worth	telescopio	telescope
mínimo	minimum	televisión	television
nacional	national	temperatura	temperature
necesario	necessary	último	ultimate
negativo	negative	unidad	unity
nervioso	nervous	urbano	urban
novela	novel	vacante	vacant
objecto	object	vena	vein
ocasión	occasion	victoria	victory
ocupado	occupied	visión	vision

Challenge

Spanish Word	English Word	Spanish Word	English Word
absoluto	absolute	auténtico	authentic
abismo	abyss	automático	automatic
absurdo	absurd	bárbaro	barbarian
acelerar	accelerate	beneficio	benefit
aceptación	acceptance	biología	biology
admiración	admiration	bulevar	boulevard
adolesencia	adolescence	calcular	calculate
ambulancia	ambulance	celebración	celebration
asociación	association	competencia	competition
astrónomo	astronomer	contribución	contribution
atracción	attraction	cooperación	cooperate

Spanish Word	English Word	Spanish Word	English Word
cuota	quota	juventud	youth
curiosidad	curiosity	lenguaje	language
decimo	tenth	majestad	majesty
defecto	defect; fault	maravilloso	marvelous
departamento	department	metropolitano	metropolitan
descender	lower	nacionalidad	nationality
destino	destiny	naturalmente	naturally
elástico	elastic	obediente	obedient
electricidad	electricity	objetivo	objective
facilidad	facility; ease	oportunidad	opportunity
facultad	faculty	pacifico	pacific; peaceful
fatiga	fatigue	pavimento	pavement
festividad	festivity	percepción	perception
fractura	fracture; break	realidad	reality
generosidad	generosity	recientemente	recently
grotesco	grotesque	recreación	recreation
habitante	inhabitant	referencia	reference
hemisferio	hemisphere	satélite	satellite
historiador	historian	sobrenatural	supernatural
hospitalidad	hospitality	solidario	solidarity; unity
humanidad	humanity	turista	tourist
imaginativo	imaginary	tradicional	traditional
imitación	imitation	tragedia	tragedy
imperativo	imperative	universidad	university
imperio	empire	vacaciones	vacation
inmediatamente	immediately	vehiculo	vehicle
justicia	justice		

BRITISH-AMERICAN WORDS AND TERMS

Even though the British and Americans share the same language, some words and phrases are different.

Easy

British Word	American Word	British Word	American Word
biscuit	cookie	mate	friend
chips	fries	mum	mom
dustbin	trash can	post	mail
flat	apartment	pram	baby carriage
football	soccer	sweets	candy
hire	rent	tap	faucet
holiday	vacation	telly	TV
jug	pitcher	tin	can
lift	elevator	trousers	pants

Target

British Word	American Word	British Word	American Word
banger	sausage	ice lolly	popsicle
banknote	bill	jello	jelly
bank cashier	teller	jelly	jam
bonnet	car hood	jumper	sweater
boot	car trunk	loo	bathroom
carrier bag	shopping bag	lorry	truck
car park	parking lot	motorway	highway
caravan	motor home; trailer	nappy	diaper
constable	police officer (especially one on foot patrol)	pavement	sidewalk
		petrol	gas
cooker	stove	plaster	band-aid
crisps	potato chips	postal code	zip code
diversion	detour	push chair	stroller
full stop	period	queue	line
		rasher	slice of bacon

British Word	American Word	British Word	American Word
row	argument	torch	flashlight
rucksack	backpack	trolley	cart
scone	biscuit	wardrobe	closet
take-away	takeout	windscreen	windshield

Challenge

British Word	American Word	British Word	American Word
aubergine	eggplant	roundabout	traffic circle
bed sit	studio apartment	rubber	eraser
braces	suspenders	runner beans	stringbeans
chemist	pharmacy	serviette	napkin
cinema	movie theater	silencer	muffler
commercial traveler	traveling salesperson	sitting room	living room
		solicitor	lawyer
draughts	checkers	surgery	doctor's office
drawing pin	thumbtack	swimming costume	bathing suit
dressing gown	robe	tea towel	dish towel
flyover	overpass	toll motorway	turnpike; toll road
fortnight	two weeks	trainers	sneakers
ground floor	first floor	turnups	cuffs
kerosene	paraffin	tube	subway
knickers	underpants	vacuum flask	thermos bottle
macintosh	raincoat	verge (of road)	shoulder
nought	nothing	waistcoat	vest
pinafore	jumper	wellies	galoshes; boots
plimsolls	gym shoes	zebra crossing	crosswalk
public school	private school		
return ticket	round-trip ticket		

Word Differences and Wordplay

> "*I'm showing my students the importance of choosing the best word when writing. I need some more examples of shades of difference among synonyms.*"

English is a very versatile language and, with the help of the lists in this chapter, it is possible for students to avoid tired words and choose the best word or phrase to make meaning clear when speaking or writing. When it's really *frosty* outside, why say it's *cold*? Why say *blue* when a more precise description may warrant *sapphire* or *indigo*? Continue to challenge students to refine their word choices and elaborate in their writing by using words that show shades of meaning.

Exploring some of the more playful aspects of language, such as regionalisms, onomatopoeia, and idioms, can foster a curiosity about language and encourage students to take more risks with their writing. You may want to invite students to illustrate or act out a favorite idiom and ask the rest of the class to identify it. Because these expressions often pose difficulties for the students who take them literally, be sure to discuss the actual meaning of an idiom and give concrete examples of when they might use it.

SHADES-OF-DIFFERENCE WORDS

English is rich in synonyms. However, synonyms are often not exactly alike. Most carry meaning under the main meaning. Finding the right word makes good writing better. It's important to understand the shades of difference in words in order to choose the best synonym to fit a context and match a purpose. In the lists below, the first word in each group has the most general meaning.

Easy

cold	below average temperature		**run**	to move at a fast pace
chilly	cold enough to make you uncomfortable or shiver		**dash**	to move quickly and suddenly
freezing	extremely cold		**jog**	to run at a slow, steady pace
frosty	cold enough to cause frost to form		**race**	to move very quickly as if in a competition
			sprint	to move quickly for a short distance
comfortable	feeling at ease and relaxed			
cozy	feeling pleasantly warm and homey		**shout**	to cry out or say something loudly
snug	feeling warm and protected		**bellow**	to shout in a deep, loud voice
			holler	to call out or shout in order to tell someone something
cry	to shed tears		**roar**	to cry out, especially in anger or excitement
bawl	to cry noisily			
sob	to make gasping sounds while crying		**talk**	to speak
weep	to cry, often quietly		**babble**	to talk without making sense
whimper	to cry weakly, make whining sounds		**chat**	to talk in a friendly and casual way
			discuss	to talk in a purposeful way, particularly in order to make a decision
mean	not nice; unkind			
cruel	deliberately unkind			
nasty	very unpleasant; spiteful		**walk**	to move by using your legs and feet
vicious	extremely cruel		**amble**	walk slowly and leisurely
old	the opposite of young		**stride**	to walk by taking long steps
ancient	very old; from the distant past		**trudge**	to walk slowly and wearily
antique	valuable because of its age, rarity, and beauty			
pretty	pleasing to look at			
beautiful	very good-looking			
cute	sweet and pleasing; delightful			
lovely	gracefully delicate and pleasing			

Target

bad	badly behaved
naughty	badly behaved and causing mischief, but without meaning serious harm
wicked	badly behaved and morally wrong
evil	foul; purposefully causing trouble
blame	find fault with or think someone responsible for a wrongdoing
accuse	charge someone with a wrongdoing or crime
criticize	point out someone's faults
denounce	speak out publicly against someone
condemn	judge that someone is guilty and deserves punishment
brave	not afraid
courageous	consciously facing danger boldly by drawing on inner strength
fearless	having no fear in the face of danger
heroic	showing the bravery and daring typical of a hero
busy	full of activity
bustling	full of energy and noise
hectic	too busy; frantic
lively	full of energy and life
cheap	not willing to give or spend money freely
economical	careful to spend money in the most advantageous way
miserly	greedy and unwilling to give or spend money
stingy	not generous; giving or spending as little money as possible
thrifty	spending money cautiously and sensibly

childlike	like a child
childish	behaving in a way more appropriate to a child than an adult
immature	not yet fully developed; not developed to a level appropriate for one's age
juvenile	appropriate for young people or children
common	not special
average	typical of a group
mundane	common and often boring
ordinary	usual and customary; not distinguishable from others
confident	behaving in a way that shows faith in yourself
aggressive	behaving in a forceful and sometimes belligerent manner
assertive	behaving in a strong, firm, and self-confident manner
cocky	behaving in an overly self-confident and arrogant manner
confuse	to mix someone or something up
puzzle	to confuse someone and make that person feel unsure
baffle	to make someone feel very confused and helpless
mystify	to make something seem too mysterious to understand
depressing	causing feelings of sadness
dreary	dull and depressing
gloomy	dark and cheerless
dismal	depressing and hopeless

disagree — to have different opinions

argue — to express different opinions, often angrily

bicker — to argue about something unimportant in a bad-tempered way

debate — to talk formally and at length about different positions

error — something that is not correct or is misunderstood

blunder — a serious or embarrassing error or mistake

gaffe — a clumsy mistake made in a social situation

mistake — an error that results from carelessness

slip — a slight mistake

friend — someone you are close to and get along with well

ally — someone you bond with for mutual aid and support to reach a shared goal

colleague — someone you work with

confederate — someone you join with to carry out a plot or conspiracy

funny — causing laughter

amusing — pleasant and entertaining

droll — funny because it is odd or strange

hilarious — very funny; causing outbursts of laughter

witty — clever, stylish, and amusing

happy — the opposite of sad

blissful — serenely happy

content — pleased and satisfied

gleeful — very happy and pleased because of something that has happened

joyous — full of great joy and happiness

intelligent — quick in thinking; able to reason effectively

bright — able to learn quickly and easily

clever — mentally quick, ingenious, and original

shrewd — showing keen judgment, particularly in business dealings and politics

smart — quick in thinking and able to take care of yourself

wise — able to make good decisions on the basis of what you know

laugh — to make sounds expressing amusement

chortle — to laugh in a noisy and gleeful way

chuckle — to laugh quietly or to yourself

giggle — to laugh quietly in a silly or childish way

snicker — to laugh in a disrespectful way

love — to care deeply about someone

adore — to love and honor someone intensely

idolize — to deeply admire and respect someone

worship — to treat someone as though that person were a god

pile — a number of things heaped together

clutter — an untidy pile of things

jumble — an untidy and disorganized pile of things

hodgepodge — a pile of unrelated things

mess — an untidy and usually dirty pile of things

polite — showing good manners

civil — polite in a cold and formal manner

courteous — polite, gracious, and considerate

well-mannered — showing proper behavior and good manners

pretend	to make believe something is true or real that isn't
bluff	to pretend something in order to trick or frighten someone
deceive	to mislead someone deliberately
feign	to fake, imitate, or copy something
rain	drops of water from the sky
drizzle	light but steady rain
pour	heavy rain
sleet	frozen rain
rude	not polite; disagreeable
coarse	displaying a lack of taste and refinement
uncouth	bad-mannered, clumsy, and graceless
unrefined	not acting in a socially acceptable way
vulgar	crude and obscene
scared	frightened; afraid
aghast	feeling shock, dismay, and alarm
horrified	feeling revulsion, disgust, and shock
terrified	feeling overpowering and often paralyzing fear
shiny	bright, glossy, and reflecting light
brilliant	extremely bright
dazzling	spectacularly bright; stunning
luminous	glowing; startlingly bright
lustrous	with a soft shine
shy	not comfortable around people
bashful	self-conscious and awkward around people
coy	pretending self-consciousness around people
diffident	reserved and restrained because of a lack of confidence
timid	nervous around people

strange	not common or usual
alien	outside normal experience
exotic	strikingly unusual and suggestive of foreign countries
foreign	from another place or country
surprise	to fill someone with sudden wonder
amaze	to make someone feel very surprised
astonish	to make someone feel overwhelmingly surprised
astound	to make someone feel extreme surprise and shock
thin	without extra fat on your body
skinny	thin in an unhealthy and unpleasant way
slender	thin in a graceful and attractive way
svelte	particularly slim and attractive
trim	slim and fit
truthful	expressing feeling and opinions in an honest way
blunt	expressing feelings and opinions freely and openly without regard for their effect on others
candid	expressing feelings and opinions in an open, sincere, and straightforward manner
frank	expressing feelings and opinions in an open, honest, and forceful way
worried	feeling concerned and troubled
agitated	worried, nervous, and upset; unable to rest
anxious	worried and afraid that something bad will happen
distraught	overly worried and distressed
hysterical	panic-stricken

Challenge

able	equipped to do something
capable	able to do a particular task
competent	having the skills necessary to do a particular task
skilled	having a special ability to do a particular task
agreement	an understanding or arrangement
accord	a treaty or settlement
consensus	general, widespread agreement
pact	an agreement to do something
annoyed	mildly disturbed or displeased
bothered	annoyed and feeling put-upon
irked	annoyed and wearied
vexed	annoyed and angered
apparent	easy to see and understand
blatant	exceedingly obvious; impossible to hide
conspicuous	easy to see because it attracts attention
obvious	easy to see and understand because nothing is hidden
average	typical
mediocre	run-of-the-mill; okay but not very good
middling	neither good nor bad
standard	up to the norm for acceptability and quality
careful	showing care; thorough
accurate	without error
meticulous	extremely careful and precise
painstaking	showing great care and attention to detail

constant	steady; always present
continual	happening again and again at regular intervals
continuous	happening without interruption for a long period of time
persistent	continuing relentlessly for a long period of time
dishonest	not honest; lying and cheating
calculating	scheming and acting in order to get the advantage
conniving	devious and scheming
deceitful	purposefully misleading or untruthful
mendacious	chronically lying
destroy	to ruin completely
annihilate	to wipe out so completely it no longer exists; to vanquish
decimate	to kill every tenth person; to kill a large part of a group/population
devastate	to cause widespread damage
slaughter	to kill brutally and mercilessly
early	ahead of time
premature	before the expected or advisable time
untimely	at a bad or inconvenient time; happening too soon
eerie	strange and frightening
gruesome	focusing on cruelty and injury in order to cause horror and shock
macabre	focusing on the horror of death and decay
morbid	dark and gloomy in an unhealthy and unwholesome way

judge	to form an opinion of someone or something
arbitrate	to act as judge in a dispute
mediate	to help both sides of a dispute reach an agreement
referee	to decide a contest, particularly in sports

pity	sorrow caused by someone else's misfortune or pain
compassion	concern for the suffering of others and a desire to help
sympathy	a feeling of sharing the suffering and pain of others
empathy	strong identification with the pain and suffering of others

praise	express approval and admiration
commend	praise in a formal way
eulogize	praise highly
extol	praise enthusiastically and with great admiration

real	not artificial
authentic	reliable; trustworthy
genuine	being what it claims to be
unadulterated	not changed in any way

shorten	to reduce the length or duration of
abbreviate	to shorten by removing parts of
abridge	to shorten by cutting parts or summarizing
truncate	to shorten by cutting off the final part

showy	making an impressive display
gaudy	loud, flashy, and extravagant
garish	crudely ornate and showy
ostentatious	pretentiously showy
tawdry	cheap and showy

usual	normal; common; ordinary
customary	conforming to established customs and procedures
habitual	done on a regular and frequent basis

ADJECTIVES THAT SHOW DEGREE

Some synonyms for adjectives compare the degree or extent of a quality, such as how much of something there is or how bad or good something is. In the lists below, the last word in each group shows the superlative.

Easy

adjective	comparative	superlative	adjective	comparative	superlative
bad	worse	worst	lukewarm	warm	hot
cool	cold	frigid	many	more	most (countable things)
good	better	best			
little	less	least	much	more	most (an amount you cannot count)

Target

adjective	comparative	superlative	adjective	comparative	superlative
big	huge	immense	necessary	essential	indispensable
full	packed	stuffed	risky	serious	critical
grand	magnificent	majestic	tired	weary	exhausted
great	terrific	superb	top	apex	zenith
greatest	maximum	ultimate	weak	feeble	decrepit
loud	ear-splitting	deafening	wild	fierce	ferocious

Challenge

adjective	comparative	superlative	adjective	comparative	superlative
difficult	challenging	grueling	plentiful	abundant	profuse
disastrous	calamitous	catastrophic	terrible	appalling	abysmal
disliked	hated	detested	unappealing	repellent	hideous
eager	enthusiastic	avid	unhappy	dejected	disconsolate
interesting	absorbing	fascinating	urgent	vital	imperative

COLOR WORDS

English is rich in words that name different shades or variations of primary and secondary colors. As a result, we can choose the exact word we need to describe a color. Some color words are derived from objects that are that precise color, such as *ruby* and *periwinkle*. Others come from words in other languages, such as *cerise* and *puce* (French).

Easy

black	brown	gray	orange	purple	rose	tan	yellow
blue	gold	green	pink	red	silver	white	

Target

apricot	pale yellowish orange
aquamarine	greenish blue
auburn	deep coppery red or reddish brown
azure	sky blue
beige	creamy brown
bronze	deep yellowish brown
buff	pale yellowish pink
canary	bright intense yellow
champagne	pale brownish gold
cherry	strong bright red to purplish red
chestnut	deep reddish brown
copper	reddish brown
coral	deep orangey pink or reddish orange
cream	pale yellow to yellowish white
crimson	deep, rich purplish red
ebony	deep brownish black
emerald	intense yellowish green
fawn	pale, soft yellowish brown
fuchsia	brilliant deep purplish pink
indigo	blue violet
ivory	pale yellowish white
khaki	light brown
lavender	pale purple
lilac	pinkish purple
magenta	brilliant reddish purple
mahogany	deep reddish brown
maroon	brownish red or purple
mauve	light pinkish purple
navy	dark blue
olive	deep yellowish green
peach	creamy yellowish orange
pearl	yellowish white
periwinkle	pale purplish blue
plum	dark reddish purple
ruby	deep, intense red tinged with purple
russet	brownish red
rust	reddish brown
sable	black or grayish, yellowish brown
saffron	deep yellowish orange
sage	grayish green
salmon	pinkish orange

sapphire	brilliant intense blue		**tawny**	light brown or brownish orange
scarlet	deep red		**teal**	greenish blue
slate	black tinged with purple or gray		**topaz**	dark brownish yellow
tangerine	bright orange or reddish orange		**turquoise**	bright greenish blue or bluish green
taupe	deep brownish gray		**violet**	deep purplish blue

Challenge

alabaster	translucent white		**heliotrope**	violet or purplish red
amethyst	bluish purple		**henna**	rich reddish brown
aubergine	dark purple		**hoary**	silvery gray or snow white
burgundy	deep red		**madder**	reddish orange
carmine	deep purplish red		**ocher**	yellowish orange or brown
celadon	pale grayish green		**perse**	dark grayish blue or purple
cerise	deep purplish red		**puce**	purplish red or pink
cerulean	sky blue		**reseda**	dull grayish green
chartreuse	intense yellowish green		**sienna**	earthy reddish brown
cinnabar	deep red tinged with orange		**sorrel**	brownish orange or light brown
citrine	dark greenish yellow		**terra cotta**	reddish brown
citron	grayish green		**titian**	bright reddish gold
claret	dark purplish red		**ultramarine**	deep brilliant blue
cyan	deep greenish blue		**umber**	earthy brown
ecru	pale grayish, yellowish brown		**vermilion**	bright red or reddish orange

EUPHEMISMS

A euphemism is a softer, blander word used in place of
a harsher, blunter word. A euphemism often covers up
an offensive or distasteful quality clearly conveyed by the
original word.

Easy

Original Word	Euphemism	Original Word	Euphemism
dead	deceased	problem	challenge
die	pass away	old age	golden years
garbage	waste	old person	senior citizen

Target

Original Word	Euphemism	Original Word	Euphemism
burial ground	cemetery; memorial park	insane asylum	sanatorium; psychiatric hospital
disabled	challenged	poor	underprivileged
garbage collector	sanitation worker	prison	correctional institution
garbage collection	waste management	rerun	encore performance
garbage dump	refuse collection area	superintendent	custodial engineer
kill	terminate	used car	preowned vehicle

Challenge

Original Word	Euphemism	Original Word	Euphemism
attack, raid	incursion	old-fashioned	retro
bathroom	facility	picky	discriminating
burial	interment	poorly behaved	maladjusted
civilian causalities	collateral damage	retreat	strategic withdrawal
crime	antisocial behavior	rude	socially maladjusted
conquer	pacify	slum	economically disadvantaged area
conquest	pacification	theft	misappropriation of funds
killed by own troops	friendly fire	war	military action
imitation	faux		
lie	fabrication		

REGIONALISMS

Many common objects are called different things in different locations or parts of the country. Words like this are called regionalisms. Sometimes the exact places where a regionalism is used may be difficult to pinpoint. Some can be isolated to one area, such as the Southeast or Midwest. Others pop up around the country in places that are far apart, such as in Boston, the Midwest, and California. In the lists below, the most commonly or widely used term is listed first.

Easy

bag	coke
poke	pop
sack	soda
	tonic

Target

drinking fountain	highway	porch	submarine (sandwich)
bubbler	freeway	gallery	Cuban sandwich
	expressway	stoop	grinder
frying pan	the I	veranda	hero
fry pan	thruway		hoagie
skillet		rubberband	Italian sandwich
spider	margarine	gumband	poor boy (or po' boy)
	oleo	elastic	
garage			
carport	milk shake	remarkable	
	frappe	bodacious	
grocery cart			
buggy	pancakes	sofa	
shopping wagon	battercakes	couch	
	flapjacks	davenport	
grocery store	griddlecakes		
bodega	hotcakes	sprinkles	
corner market	johnnycakes	jimmies	
mini-mart			

Challenge

andiron	orphaned calf	traffic circle	valley
dog iron	dogie	rotary	hollow
		roundabout	
detergent	squad car	turn signal	
washing powder	cruiser	blinker	
	patrol car	directional signal	
gazebo	prowl car		
belvedere			
pagoda			
summerhouse			
garden folly			

ONOMATOPOEIA WORDS

Some words imitate sounds. They can be the sounds made by animals, people, or things. You would think these words would be standard from language to language, but they are not. For example, in English a cat says, "meow," in Danish, "mjav," in Japanese, "nyaa," and in Bengali, "meu."

Easy

baa	clop	moo	tick-tock
beep	cock-a-doodle-doo	neigh	tweet
boo-hoo	ding-dong	oink	whoo
bow-wow	gobble	ouch	woof
buzz	hee-haw	peep	
choo choo	meow	quack	

Target

achoo	coo	plop	thud
arf	crackle	pow	thump
bong	croak	ribbit	twitter
bonk	crunch	screech	wham
brr	duh	smack	whinny
burp	eek	snarl	whoosh
chirp	fizz	snort	whizz
clang	growl	splash	yelp
clickety clack	grr	splat	zap
clink	hiss	squawk	
clip clop	jingle	squeal	
clunk	mew	swoosh	

Challenge

ahem	caw	pitter-patter	twang
argh	cha-ching	poof	vroom
baroom	gurgle	rustle	whiffle
blah blah blah	hmmm	sizzle	yadda yadda yadda
bleet	humph	slurp	yahoo
boing	ka-boom	thunk	
bray	mumble	tsk-tsk	

NOUNS AND ADJECTIVES FOR ANIMALS

Many of the names of animals are based on Old English words. Often we form an adjective by adding a suffix to the noun. Sometimes, though, an adjective is formed from the Latin word for the animal. For example, a dog displays canine behavior. Usually, the Latin form of the adjective carries the meaning "relating to or characteristic of" and has a more scientific application.

Easy

noun	adjective	adjective (Latin form)	noun	adjective	adjective (Latin form)
cat	catty	feline	horse	horsy	equine
dog	doggish	canine			

Target

noun	adjective	adjective (Latin form)	noun	adjective	adjective (Latin form)
ape	ape-like	simian	lion	lion-like	leonine
bee	bee-like	apian	monkey	monkey-like	simian
bird	bird-like	avian	rabbit	rabbity	lapine
bull	bullish	taurine	snake	snakelike	serpentine
cow	cow-like	bovine	spider	spidery	arachnoid
donkey	donkey-like	asinine	pig	piggish	porcine
fish	fishy	piscine	wolf	wolfish	lupine

Challenge

noun	adjective	adjective (Latin form)	noun	adjective	adjective (Latin form)
badger	badger-like	musteline	hare	hare-like	leporine
bear	bearish	ursine	hog	hoggish	suilline
calf	calf-like	vituline	lizard	lizard-like	saurian
deer	deer-like	cervine	rodent	rodent-like	murine
eagle	eagle-like	aquiline	sheep	sheep-like	ovine
fox	foxy	vulpine	squirrel	squirrelly	sciurine
goat	goaty	caprine	worm	wormy	vermian

PALINDROMES

Palindromes are words that read the same backward and forward.

Easy

bib	hah	pep	sis
dad	mom	pip	tat
deed	noon	pop	tot
did	pap	pup	toot
eye	peep	sees	wow

Target

aha	eve	ma'am	shahs
civic	gag	madam	solos
denned	gig	pull up	
dewed	kook	put up	
eke	level	redder	

Challenge

deified	repaper	sagas
kayak	reviver	stats
race car	rotator	tenet
radar	rotor	

IDIOMS

An idiom is a group of words that takes on a special meaning that is different from the meaning of each individual word. These expressions are easy for native speakers to understand but pose difficulties for nonnative speakers, who tend to take them literally. Idioms are often fresh and colorful, but when they become overused, they become cliches.

Easy

Idiom	Meaning	Example of Idiom	Example of Meaning
an arm and a leg	a great deal; a lot of money	The present cost an arm and a leg.	The present cost a lot of money.
apple of one's eye	someone or something one adores or likes a lot	Janina was the apple of her father's eye.	Janina was adored by her father.
a bee in one's bonnet	something you can't help thinking about	She had a bee in her bonnet about getting a kitten.	She couldn't help thinking about getting a kitten.
catch cold	contract or develop a cold	Dress warmly so that you don't catch cold.	Dress warmly so that you don't develop a cold.
catch one's breath	to rest	The acrobats didn't have time to catch their breath between acts.	The acrobats didn't have time to rest between acts.
cry wolf	give a false alarm	If you cry wolf too often, people won't pay attention when you are really in trouble.	If you give a false alarm too often, people won't pay attention when you are really in trouble.
drop the ball	fail to do something	I was depending on her to order the supplies, but at the last minute she dropped the ball.	I was depending on her to order the supplies, but at the last minute she failed to do it.
have one's cake and eat it too	use something but still have it	She couldn't decide whether to spend money on the sweater or not, since she wanted to have her cake and eat it too.	She couldn't decide whether to spend money on the sweater or not, since she wanted to buy the sweater but also keep the money.

Idiom	Meaning	Example of Idiom	Example of Meaning
feather in one's cap	reward; honor; prize	For Anita, winning the soccer game was a feather in her cap.	For Anita, winning the soccer game was an honor.
get cold feet	lose one's nerve	Jack got cold feet and didn't ask Eliza to the concert.	Jack lost his nerve and didn't ask Eliza to the concert.
get up on the wrong side of bed	be in a bad mood	"Stay out of his way," said Chris, "since it looks like he got up on the wrong side of bed."	"Stay out of his way," said Chris, "since he's in a bad mood."
hands down	easily; without effort	The team won the soccer game hands down.	The team won the soccer game easily.
head over heels	completely; overwhelmingly	In the movie, the two stars were head over heels in love.	In the movie, the two stars were overwhelmingly in love.
keep one's fingers crossed	hope	Keep your fingers crossed that I pass the tryouts.	Hope that I pass the tryouts.
last straw	final annoyance	Your eating my piece of pie is the last straw. I won't put up with your behavior anymore.	Your eating my piece of pie is the final annoyance. I won't put up with your behavior anymore.
lend a hand	help	Please lend me a hand with my chores.	Please help me with my chores.
let the cat out of the bag	let a secret be known	Be careful you don't let the cat out of the bag and tell her about the surprise party.	Be careful you don't let her know the secret and tell her about the surprise party.
make up something	create; fib or lie	The little boy made up a story to explain the missing cookies.	The little boy fibbed to explain the missing cookies.
on the ball	alert; competent	The new coach was certainly on the ball; he didn't miss anything.	The new coach was certainly alert; he didn't miss anything.
picture of (something)	perfect example of	When she won the blue ribbon, she was the picture of happiness.	When she won the blue ribbon, she was a perfect example of happiness.

Idiom	Meaning	Example of Idiom	Example of Meaning
piece of cake	very easy	After studying so hard, getting an A on the test was a piece of cake.	After studying so hard, getting an A on the test was very easy.
pull one's leg	tease; fool or trick	Uncle James didn't mean it; he was just pulling your leg.	Uncle James didn't mean it; he was just teasing you.
put the cart before the horse	do something in the wrong order	Getting paid before you do the chore is putting the cart before the horse	Getting paid before you do the chore is the wrong order.
ring a bell	remind of something	That name doesn't ring a bell.	That name doesn't remind me of anything.
take a catnap	sleep for a short period of time	Lisa took a catnap before going to the movies.	Lisa slept for a short period of time before going to the movies.

Target

Idiom	Meaning	Example of Idiom	Example of Meaning
ball is in your court	is your turn to do something	"I've made my final offer," the CEO said, "and now the ball is in your court."	"I've made my final offer," the CEO said, "and now it's your turn to do something."
bark up the wrong tree	follow the wrong course of action	The reporter who followed a false lead was barking up the wrong tree.	The reporter who followed a false lead was following the wrong course of action.
beat around the bush	avoid talking about a topic	Leslie was embarrassed so she tried to beat around the bush.	Leslie was embarrassed so she tried to avoid talking about the problem.
breathe a word of	tell anyone	Don't breathe a word of this to the newspapers.	Don't tell the newspapers.
bite the hand that feeds you	harm someone who helps you	Be careful what you say about your advisor. Remember that you shouldn't bite the hand that feeds you.	Be careful what you say about your advisor. Remember that you shouldn't harm someone who helps you.

Idiom	Meaning	Example of Idiom	Example of Meaning
catch red-handed	catch someone in the midst of committing a crime or another wrongdoing	The police caught the thief red-handed.	The police caught the thief in the midst of committing the crime.
come out in the wash	work out all right	Stick with it and your problems will all come out in the wash.	Stick with it and your problems will all work out all right.
cover a lot of ground	discuss a lot of topics	Let's get started right away since we have to cover a lot of ground in this meeting.	Let's get started right away since we have to discuss a lot of topics in this meeting.
face the music	accept punishment or unpleasant consequences	The defendant confessed and was resolved to face the music.	The defendant confessed and was resolved to accept punishment.
fighting chance	good chance or possibility	She had a fighting chance of winning the election.	She had a good chance of winning the election.
from the bottom of one's heart	sincerely	I thank you from the bottom of my heart.	I thank you sincerely.
get off on the wrong foot	begin badly	Don't get off on the wrong foot by doing something foolish on the first day of school.	Don't begin badly by doing something foolish on the first day of school.
get off to a flying start	begin well	The guests were all excited to be there, and the party got off to a flying start.	The guests were all excited to be there, and the party began well.
go overboard	do too much; be excessive	Don't go overboard when buying treats for the party.	Don't be excessive when buying treats for the party.
go to the dogs	ruin; deteriorate badly	The aging actor was fearful of letting his appearance go to the dogs.	The aging actor was fearful of letting his appearance deteriorate badly.
have egg on one's face	be embarrassed because of an error	Layla had egg on her face after she realized her mistake.	Layla was embarrassed after she realized her mistake.
have second thoughts	have doubts about	Jaime had second thoughts about buying that computer game.	Jaime had doubts about buying that computer game.

Idiom	Meaning	Example of Idiom	Example of Meaning
hit the nail on the head	be exactly right	You hit the nail on the head with that answer.	You were exactly right with that answer.
knocked off one's feet	overwhelmingly surprised	Since my sister is away at college, I was knocked off my feet when she showed up at my birthday party.	Since my sister is away at college, I was overwhelmingly surprised when she showed up at my birthday party.
off the hook	freed from obligations or responsibility	Since Yolanda agreed to take over the job, you are off the hook.	Since Yolanda agreed to take over the job, you are freed from responsibility.
once in a blue moon	rarely	A streak of luck like that happens only once in a blue moon.	A streak of luck like that happens only rarely.
par for the course	usual; typical	During the winter months, it was par for the course for three or four students to be out sick.	During the winter months, it was usual for three or four students to be out sick.
raise eyebrows	make others surprised or feel disapproval	The way the star was dressed was bound to raise some eyebrows.	The way the star was dressed was bound to make some people disapprove.
snake in the grass	a treacherous person	He posed as his friend, but he was really a snake in the grass waiting for the opportunity to betray him.	He posed as his friend, but he was really a treacherous person waiting for the opportunity to betray him.
don't waste your breath	don't bother to say something because it won't make a difference.	Don't waste your breath trying to convince him to change his vote.	Don't bother to try to convince him to change his vote because it won't make a difference.

Challenge

Idiom	Meaning	Example of Idiom	Example of Meaning
bend one's ear	talk too much to someone; be overly chatty and annoying	At the dinner party, the person on my left bent my ear all night, telling me about his problems.	At the dinner party, the person on my left talked too much and annoyed me, telling me about his problems.
eye of the storm	center of a problem or controversy	The candidate found herself in the eye of the storm.	The candidate found herself in the center of the controversy.
feet of clay	have hidden faults	The reporter set out to prove that the esteemed politician really had feet of clay.	The reporter set out to prove that the esteemed politician really had hidden faults.
green-light a project	give approval for a project to move ahead	The board of directors decided to green-light the project.	The board of directors decided to give approval for the project to move ahead.
give someone a blank check	let someone spend as much as necessary; unlimited funds	The business tycoon gave the relief organization a blank check to provide housing for the flood victims.	The business tycoon gave the relief organization unlimited funds to provide housing for the flood victims.
have a bone to pick	have a matter to discuss or argue about	After reading her comment in the newspaper, he stormed into her office and said, "I have a bone to pick with you."	After reading her comment in the newspaper, he stormed into her office and said, "I have a matter to discuss with you."
have a vested interest in	be personally interested in	As your mentor, I have a vested interest in your success.	As your mentor, I am personally interested in your success.
heartbeat away from	extremely close to; next in line for	He was a heartbeat away from winning the presidency.	He was extremely close to winning the presidency.
horse of a different color	completely new and different	The solution you just proposed is a horse of a different color.	The solution you just proposed is completely new and different.

Idiom	Meaning	Example of Idiom	Example of Meaning
in a dead heat	tied	At the end of the show, the two contestants were in a dead heat.	At the end of the show, the two contestants were tied.
in one fell swoop	in one swift action	In one fell swoop, the company closed down 20 plants across the country.	In one swift action, the company closed down 20 plants across the county.
in the black	making money	The new company president is credited with strategies that made the company operate in the black.	The new company president is credited with strategies that made the company operate successfully and make money.
in the red	losing money	The books show that the company is in the red.	The books show that the company is losing money.
jog one's memory	help one remember	Does this note jog your memory?	Does this note help you remember?
lesser of two evils	the better of two poor choices	Neither option was what she wanted, but she picked the lesser of two evils.	Neither option was what she wanted, but she picked the better of two poor choices.
make allowances for	consider something when making a decision or doing something; take into consideration	The judges made allowances for the age differences of the contestants.	The judges considered the age differences of the contestants.
meeting of minds	reach agreement	After arguing for several hours, they had a meeting of minds.	After arguing for several hours, they reached agreement.
on a shoestring	with very little money	They started their business on a shoestring.	They started their business with very little money.
opening gambit	something said or done to secure a position or advantage	As an opening gambit, she said she would increase health-care benefits for all employees.	To secure her position, she said at the beginning that she would increase health-care benefits for all employees.

Idiom	Meaning	Example of Idiom	Example of Meaning
out of one's depth	involved in something that is too difficult	The newly promoted executive felt out of his depth when the employees went on strike.	The newly promoted executive was involved in something that was too difficult for him to handle when the employees went on strike.
put a spin on	twist something to one's advantage	His supporters put a spin on the results from the poll.	His supporters twisted the results from the poll to his advantage.
put to bed	complete work on and send off	They put the newspaper to bed and sent it off to the presses.	They completed work on the newspaper and sent it off to the presses.
read loud and clear	understand something that was said completely	You don't have to keep hinting about what present you want, since I read you loud and clear.	You don't have to keep hinting about what present you want, since I understand what you said completely.
shed light on	help someone understand something	The students asked the teacher to shed light on the problem.	The students asked the teacher to help them understand the problem.
shot in the dark	wild guess	We didn't really know the answer, but we took a shot in the dark.	We didn't really know the answer, but we took a wild guess.
stand on ceremony	wait for a formal invitation	Rosalie didn't stand on ceremony but went up and introduced herself to the government official.	Rosalie didn't wait for a formal invitation but went up and introduced herself to the government official.

WORDS THAT COME IN NONREVERSIBLE PAIRS

Some idiomatic expressions are made up of word pairs that always occur in a certain order. Sometimes the two words in the pair are separated by the word *and* or *or*.

Easy

back and forth	huff and puff	over and under
black and blue	knick-knack	up and down
cat and mouse	in and out	upside down

Target

an arm and a leg	high and low	question and answer
around and about	hot and cold	rain or shine
bells and whistles	in and out	sink or swim
better or worse	life and death	sooner or later
bow and arrow	last in, first out	straight and narrow
do or die	loud and clear	to and fro
down and dirty	make or break	tooth and nail
down and out	odds and ends	topsy-turvy
far and away	over and out	touch and go
far and wide	over and under	wear and tear
give and take	pins and needles	willy-nilly
head over heels	pros and cons	

Challenge

aches and pains	fast and furious	life and death
all or nothing	first and foremost	nuts and bolts
armed and dangerous	flotsam and jetsam	onward and upward
be all and end all	hale and hearty	rant and rave
blood and guts	hard-and-fast	sick and tired
bread and circuses	hem and haw	take it or leave it
by and large	high and dry	straight and narrow
cap and gown	house and home	trials and tribulations
cease and desist	hurly-burly	up-and-coming
crash and burn	hoity-toity	wax and wane
crimson and clover	kith and kin	
dog and pony show	law and order	

TWO-PART VERBS

Some verbs form an idiom when followed by an adverb or preposition. This type of two-part verb is called a phrasal.

Easy

add up	hear of	show up
back down	hold on	slow down
back up	lie down	slow up
go over	put on	
hear from	run away	

Target

break down	catch up	take after
bring on	dress down	take back
bring out	dress up	take down
burn down	give back	take in
burn up	give up	talk back
get around	look after	talk over
call off	point out	throw away
call up	pull out	throw out
calm down	pull through	turn into
carry on	rinse off	try on
carry out	save up	try out
catch on	send over	wash up

Challenge

bear up	drop off	see through
brush off	drop out	stand by
burn out	fall through	think over
buy out	hand down	think through
buy up	hand over	turn into
clean out	hold off	wear down
close down	make over	wear off
die down	play down	wear out
die off	push across	work out
drop by	rule out	

Jargon and Technical Words

Every field has its own jargon or special language. It is made up of the technical terms used in that field and the special meanings given to everyday terms.

This chapter provides lists of words used in different professions. One of the goals of these lists is to help students understand that some words have special meanings that are different from their everyday meanings. For example, the noun *beat* is usually understood as the regular rhythm of a piece of music or of one's heart. However, the area or subject that a newspaper reporter covers is also called a *beat*.

You may wish to use some of these words to illustrate other concepts. Include *crescendo, soprano,* or *a cappella* in a discussion about the influences other languages have had on English. Try *antibiotics, micro-organism, abnormal,* or *malnutrition* when discussing Greek and Latin prefixes. Or, even use *fastball, ballpark,* or *home plate* in a lesson about compound words.

BUSINESS WORDS

Easy

budget	employer	manufacture	staff
company	expense	plant	supervisor
cost	instruction manual	product	tax
customer	loan	profit	value
debt	loss	salary	wage
employee	manager	service	workforce

Target

accounting	competition	interview	promotion
advertising	corporation	investment	proposal
agenda	counterfeit	marketing	résumé
assembly line	credit	nonprofit organization	retail
balance sheet	deduction	overhead	revenue
benefits	earnings	patent	service industry
bond	finance	payroll	stock
brochure	flyer	press release	stockholder
capital	forecast	principal	
checking account	interest	procedure	

Challenge

accounts payable	bottom line	CPA (certified public accountant)	liquidity
accounts receivable	buy-out		net
accrual	cash flow	depreciation	operating income
allocation	CEO (chief executive officer)	equity	portfolio
annual report asset		gross	proprietor
audit	CFO (chief financial officer)	insurance	stock option
bankruptcy		inventory	subsidiary
billing	commission	leverage	turnover
board of directors	commodity	liability	

MEDIA WORDS

Easy

actor	cut	newspaper	schedule
artist	design	performer	script
artwork	DVD (digital video disc)	photography	set
audience	director	plot	setting
camera	focus	prime time	special effects
character	movie	prop	studio
costume		recording	theater

Target

acoustics	documentary	multimedia	propaganda
archive	editing	multiplex	ratings
brand	fade	narration	real time
cable	format	network	realistic
cinema	frame	option	sound effects
broadcast	genre	pan	treatment
clip art	image	perspective	voice-over
commercial	long shot	photo-realism	wipe
cropping	long take	point of view	wrap
disc	mainstream	production	zoom
dissolve	mix	projection	

Challenge

aesthetics	cinematography	HDTV (high-definition television)	public domain
analog	continuity	melodrama	repertoire
articulation	demographics	morphing	synergy
avant-garde	deregulation	niche	verisimilitude
biopic	digital	objectivity	vertical integration
broadband	docudrama	persona	
censorship	focal length		

COMPUTER WORDS AND TECHNOLOGY WORDS

Easy

back up	data	input	paste
bookmark	directory	Internet	search
boot	document	offline	server
byte	drag	online	software
clip art	e-mail	menu	store
command	font	monitor	tab
control key	format	output	Web site
cursor	keyboard	password	window

Target

blog	emoticon	network	URL (universal resource locator)
browser	header	pixel	virus
bulletin board	host	platform	Web log
cache	hypertext	program	wikibook
database	keyword	programmer	worm
digital	interface	search engine	
domain	link	spam	
download	modem	threaded discussion	

Challenge

bandwidth	file extension	metasearch engine	plug-in
Boolean operators	FTP (file transfer protocol)	netiquette	spider
CGI (common gateway interface)	HTML (hypertext markup language)	netware	Web crawler
CSE (custom search engine)	ISP (Internet service provider)	newsgroup	XML (extensible markup language)
cookie	list server	packet jam	
cyberspace		PDF (portable document format)	
		phish	

GEOGRAPHY WORDS

Easy

agriculture	forest	lake	resource
axis	fossil	latitude	sphere
canyon	gas	lava	temperature
climate	geographer	longitude	tundra
compass	globe	ocean	valley
coast	grasslands	peninsula	wetlands
continent	habitat	pond	
desert	hemisphere	prairie	
equator	island	region	

Target

acid rain	erosion	landform	projection
arid	eruption	landslide	rift valley
arroyo	extinction	layer	savanna
atmosphere	fault	magma	sedimentary
bedrock	fissure	mantle	seismograph
bog	geological era	mesa	smog
butte	geologist	metamorphic	steppe
canyon	geyser	meteor	strait
core	glacier	meteorite	tectonic plates
crater	global warming	mineral	temperate
crust	gorge	mudslide	terrain
delta	greenhouse gases	permafrost	volcano
dormant	groundwater	plate	watershed
earthquake	iceberg	plateau	weathering
epicenter	igneous	precipitation	

Challenge

accretion	bituminous	geopolitical	paleontologist
aquifer	cartographer	lithosphere	plate tectonics
archipelago	climatic zone	loam	strata
atoll	crevasse	loess	topography
bayou	deposition	megapolis	tributary
biodegradable	escarpment	moraine	trilobite
biome	estuary	nebula	

MUSIC WORDS

Easy

alto	flat	quartet	sharp
bass	instrument	quintet	solo
bar	key	rest	soprano
chorus	lyrics	rhythm	staff
duet	note	scale	trio

Target

baritone	harmony	mode	rondo
brass instruments	interlude	octave	score
chord	interval	orchestra	sequence
clef	keyboard	percussion instruments	string instruments
composer	measure	pitch	tempo
conductor	medium	range	tenor
dynamics	melody	refrain	treble
ensemble	meter	register	woodwinds

Challenge

a cappella	crescendo	mezzo forte	signature
adagio	diminuendo	mezzo piano	syncopation
allegro	forte	mezzo soprano	tonic
andante	fugue	piano	
chromatic scale	moderato	pianissimo	
coda	modulation	presto	

HEALTH WORDS

Easy

ache	cold	flu	muscle
bandage	cough	heart	pain
blood	cure	injury	patient
bone	cut	limb	skeleton
checkup	diet	lung	tooth
chest	disease	medicine	wound

Target

abnormal	carbohydrate	infectious	respiratory system
addiction	cartilage	injection	reproduction system
allergy	contagious	joint	skeletal system
artery	chronic	ligament	specialist
asthma	digestive system	lymphatic system	spinal cord
bacteria	disorder	malnutrition	stress
bladder	endocrine system	medication	surgery
blood cell	fatigue	microbe	temperature
blood pressure	fungus	muscular system	tendon
blood vessel	general practitioner	nervous system	tissue
calcium	gland	nutrition	trauma
capillary	hormone	operation	vaccination
circulatory system	immune system	prescription	vein
cancer	immunity	protein	virus

Challenge

AIDS (acquired immune deficiency syndrome)	bulimia	HIV (human immune deficiency virus	obesity
	cardiovascular		pathogen
	cholesterol	intravenous	protozoa
anorexia	communicable disease	irritant	psychiatry
antibody	congestion	malignant	psychology
antibiotic	dehydration	metabolism	psychotherapy
antigen	DNA (deoxyribonucleic acid)	microorganism	syndrome
autoimmune disease		mucus	
bronchia	esophagus	noninvasive	

ART WORDS

Easy

color	light	sculpture	wavy
curve	line	shadow	zigzag
diagonal	horizontal	space	
drawing	painting	spiral	
figure	statue	vertical	

Target

abstract	architecture	background	column
arch	acrylic	collage	complementary color

composition	hue	mural	secondary color
design	interior	oil paint	texture
dimension	landscape	palette	three-dimensional
dome	minaret	panorama	two-dimensional
exterior	mobile	pastel	watercolor
foreground	motif	photography	
harmony	mosaic	primary color	

Challenge

aesthetics	diptych	grotesque	perspective
allegory	egg tempura	impressionism	performance art
assemblage	engraving	installation	positive space
batik	etching	kinetic	realism
Byzantine	expressionism	luminosity	relief
ceramics	fauvism	minimalism	symmetry
chiaroscuro	flying buttress	negative space	
conceptual art	fresco	nonrepresentational	
cubism	gothic	opacity	

MEASUREMENT WORDS

Easy

cup	length	quart	volume
day	mile	ruler	weight
depth	minute	tape measure	width
foot	month	tablespoon	yard
gallon	ounce	teaspoon	year
hour	pint	time	
inch	pound	ton	

Target

acre	degree	line segment	percentage
angle	estimation	linear	ratio
balance	Fahrenheit	liter	temperature
capacity	fraction	meter	U.S. customary system
Celsius	gram	metric system	vertex
centimeter	kilogram	milliliter	
decimal	kilometer	millimeter	

Challenge

acceleration	dram	kelvin	peck
ampere	equivalence	lumen	rod
angstrom	farad	luminance	scale
apothecary weight	furlong	lux	square
candela	gill	metric ton	tesla
conversion	hectare	mole	velocity
coulomb	henry	newton	volt
cubic	hertz	ohm	watt
density	joule	pascal	weber

SPORTS WORDS

Easy

ballpark	coach	pass	pitcher
base	glove	shin guards	umpire
batter	kick	spikes	
bleachers	mask	team	
block	mitt	trainer	

Target

arena	fastball	kickoff	signal
backcourt	fly ball	infield	stadium
baseline	foul	inning	strike
block	forward	league	tackle
bullpen	frontcourt	leftfield	timeout
bunt	fumble	lineup	touchdown
centerfield	goalie	match	tournament
court	goal line	offense	traveling
curveball	goaltender	outfield	underdog
defense	halfback	punt	winger
down	halftime	quarterback	
dribble	home plate	referee	
dugout	home run	right field	

Challenge

battery	gridiron	pigskin	relief pitcher
blitz	interception	pinch hitter	rosin
defensive	offensive	point spread	rotation
designated hitter	on deck	possession	slider
double-team	penalty box	reception	zone defense

WRITERS ON WORDS

Easy

"When I use a word," Humpty Dumpty said, in a rather scornful tone, "it means just what I choose it to mean—neither more nor less."
"The question is," said Alice, "whether you can make words mean so many different things."
"The question is," said Humpty Dumpty, "which is to be master—that's all."

—LEWIS CARROLL

Sticks and stones may break our bones, but words will break our hearts.

—ROBERT FULGHUM

Target

All words are pegs to hang ideas on.

—HENRY WARD BEECHER

Often when I write, I am trying to make words do the work of line and colour. I have the painter's sensitivity to light. Much (perhaps the best) of my writing is verbal painting.

—ELIZABETH BOWEN

Writing cannot express all words, words cannot encompass all ideas.

—CONFUCIUS

Words are the thread on which we string our experiences.

—ALDOUS HUXLEY

Gradually from naming an object we advance step by step until we have traversed the vast distance between our first stammered syllable and the sweep of thought in a line of Shakespeare.

—HELEN KELLER

The difference between the almost right word and the right word is really a large matter—'tis the difference between the lightning bug and the lightning.

—MARK TWAIN

The English language is nobody's special property. It is the property of the imagination; it is the property of the language itself.
—Derek Walcott

Challenge

Words are things, and a small drop of ink, falling like dew upon a thought, produces that which makes thousands, perhaps millions, think.

—LORD BYRON

A word is not a crystal, transparent and unchanged, it is the skin of a living thought, and may vary greatly in color and content according to the circumstances and the time in which it is used.

—JUSTICE OLIVER WENDELL HOLMES

Words are . . . the most powerful drug used by mankind.

—RUDYARD KIPLING

Words have weight, sound and appearance; it is only by considering these that you can write a sentence that is good to look at and good to listen to.

—W. SOMERSET MAUGHAM

Wit has truth in it; wisecracking is simply calisthenics with words.

—DOROTHY PARKER

. . . I . . . believe that words can help us move or keep us paralyzed, and that our choices of language and verbal tone have something—a great deal—to do with how we live our lives and whom we end up speaking with and hearing; and that we can deflect words, by trivialization, of course, but also by ritualized respect, or we can let them enter our souls and mix with the juices of our minds."

—ADRIENNE RICH

Notes

Notes